THE LITERARY BIOGRAPHY

The Literary Biography

Problems and Solutions

Edited by

Dale Salwak

Ψ

University of Iowa Press, Iowa City

University of Iowa Press, Iowa City 52242

International Standard Book Number 0–87745–553–8

Library of Congress Catalog Card Number 95–62101

01 00 99 98 97 96 C 5 4 3 2 1

Printed in Great Britain

ABA-5839

For Edwin A. (Eddie) and Amy Dawes

Contents

Preface

This book brings together nineteen essays, the majority of them written especially for the occasion, on what has been called 'the most delicate and humane of all the branches of the art of writing'[1] – the biography, in this instance, the *literary* biography. Included in this genre are not only books with the life of a writer as their focus but also, as Justin Kaplan argues, any book that possesses literary merit, that attempts to stimulate a reader's imagination through 'the magic of language.'[2] Ranging from an examination of the traditional biographical form, which studies in detail the relation of a writer's art to his or her life, to psychobiography, which is guided by psychological theory, the essays in this volume explore the myriad ways a literary biographer approaches the craft, the immense complexities involved in recounting a life, and some possible solutions to the dilemmas that arise in the process.

As several of the contributors acknowledge, the biographer faces many challenges, among them the limitations and constraints of the chosen form. No matter how many letters, diaries, unpublished manuscripts, earlier biographies, memoirs, photographs, and other sources are available to the researcher, there remain what Victoria Glendinning calls 'lies and silences'[3] in the public record. 'Biography is the clothes and buttons of the man,' wrote Mark Twain, 'but the real biography of a man is lived in his head twenty-four hours a day, and *that* you can never know.'[4] Unlike the novel, here omniscience is impossible. There's so much that can never be known, and finding those bounds can be both daunting and intriguing.

Other obstacles confronting the biographer stem from the faulty memories of interviewees, the inability to verify facts or documents, conflicting accounts of the same events, problems of copyright, and publishers who increasingly want less rather than more detail. Construction also poses a special challenge. What shape shall the book take? Straight narrative? Topical treatment? Essay? Where should the story begin? And how should it end? What is the biographer's proper relationship with the subject? These matters, and many others, are covered in the essays that follow. 'Never mind if one has met these questions before, and answered them,' says Catherine Drinker Bowen. 'Each book one writes is different in content and therefore in form; with each book old problems present themselves in guises new and strange.'[5]

Writing about authors whose lives are over is itself difficult. But writing about living authors presents its own set of problems, including the subject's natural anxiety over the biographer's scrutiny, the seemingly endless research necessary to keep current with the primary and secondary works, the possible loss of objectivity, the perils of misinformation and miscommunication, and a lack of closure. Many biographers have experienced the frustration of not being able to consult restricted material because the author, friends, or family are understandably concerned about harmful ramifications. When writing about Sir Kingsley Amis, for example, I approached (with the author's permission) the Bodleian Library about reading Amis's letters to Philip Larkin for 'ideas', not for personal information, but was told this would not be possible. 'They are so very personal,' one librarian wrote, 'that even if Sir Kingsley himself did not mind them being read, the people he wrote about certainly would. Unfortunately, this is one of the hazards of working in the modern field where most of what one writes on a living author is bound to be provisional.'[6]

Opening the door to private lives clearly raises ethical and legal questions as well. How far should biographers go in respecting the privacy of the subject – or of other people implicated in the lives they describe? Are private lives always relevant to biography? Is it ethical to disregard instructions in documents left by the dead, even more to use those documents as a basis for further diagnosis? Surely the biographer has a responsibility in the selection of evidence: eye-witness *vs* gossip or hearsay, the scrupulous weighing of facts *vs* the preference for conjecture, and so on. 'It is the experience of many of my friends,' wrote one contributor to this volume, 'that often their giving witness to an error of fact is greeted by a biographer as an outrageous attempt to interfere with his or her creativity, as if his creation of a legend is more important than the facts of the lives he describes.' Such public *vs* private issues become all the more troubling now that many biographers are no longer unwilling to explore intimate questions of gender, race, culture and sexuality. John Updike laments, 'The trouble with literary biographies, perhaps, is that they mainly testify to the long worldly corruption of a life, as documented deeds and days and disappointments pile up, and cannot convey the unearthly human innocence that attends, in the perpetual present tense of living, the self that seems the real one.'[7]

What, then, does it take to understand another human being and then convey that understanding to the reader in a way that is humanely truthful? In the preface to her life of Frank Lloyd Wright, Meryle

Secrest paraphrases Somerset Maugham: 'There are three rules for writing biography, but, unfortunately, no one knows what they are.' Elsewhere she says, 'The biographer's overwhelming obligation is to make his subject human, and to do that he must be subtle, shrewd and knowledgeable.' According to Leon Edel, 'The biographer may be as imaginative as he pleases – the more imaginative the better – *but he must not imagine the materials.'*[8]

Given the huge number of literary biographies published annually and the controversies ignited by many of them, this volume makes a contribution to the ever-expanding dialogue on the nature of the genre, its approaches and methodologies. One of my personal motives for bringing this collection together in the first place was that I wanted to learn from the efforts of others. I have done that, and I hope the reader will as well.

DALE SALWAK

Citrus College
Glendora, California

Acknowledgements

Grateful acknowledgement is made to the following for permission to reprint previously published materials:

Antony Alpers, John Johnson Ltd and the editor for 'Biography – The "Scarlet Experiment",' *Times Literary Supplement*, 28 March 1980, pp. 369–70;

Linda H. Davis and the editor for 'The Red Room: Stephen Crane and Me,' *The American Scholar*, LXIV (1995) 1–14;

Justin Kaplan and the editor for 'A Culture of Biography,' *Yale Review*, CXXXII (1994) 1–12;

Elizabeth Longford, Alfred A. Knopf and Weidenfeld & Nicolson for 'Reflections of a Biographer,' excerpted from *The Pebbled Shore: The Memoirs of Elizabeth Longford* (1986);

Diane Wood Middlebrook, Georges Borchardt Inc. and the editor for 'Spinning Straw into Gold,' *Stanford Alumni Magazine*, June 1991, pp. 47–9;

Andrew Motion and the editor for 'Breaking In,' *Granta*, XLI (1993) 167–71;

Natasha Spender and the editor for 'Private and Public Lives,' *Times Literary Supplement*, 9 October 1992, pp. 13–14.

Every effort has been made to trace all copyright-holders, but if any have been inadvertently overlooked the publishers will be pleased to make the necessary arrangement at the first opportunity.

Notes on the Contributors

Catherine Aird is the author of seventeen detective novels, the latest of which is *After Effects,* and of a collection of her short stories called *Injury Time.* She has edited a number of parish histories and has produced both a *son et lumière* and a video on local subjects. She is presently working on a biography of Josephine Tey. She is a past chairman of the Crime Writers' Association.

Antony Alpers was Professor of English at Queen's University, Kingston, Ontario. In addition to his 1953 study of Mansfield, he is the author of *Dolphins: The Myth and the Mammal, Maori Myths and Tribal Legends, Legends of the South Seas,* and *The Life of Katherine Mansfield.*

Anthony Curtis retired as literary editor of *The Financial Times* in 1990 to concentrate on writing. He is the author of several books about Somerset Maugham. He is currently at work on *Lit. Ed.* – a book about reviewing and books pages.

Linda H. Davis has been a full-time writer since 1981. She is the author of *Onward and Upward: A Biography of Katharine S. White,* and of a forthcoming biography of Stephen Crane. Her essays have appeared in *The New Yorker, The American Scholar, The Christian Science Monitor* and other publications.

Russell Fraser is Austin Warren Professor of English Literature and Language (Emeritus) at the University of Michigan. He has published fifteen books and over 100 essays. His greatest interest is the short poem in English, and Shakespeare. Currently he is writing *Poets in English, 1500 to the Present.* He has also taught at Duke, Vanderbilt University (as Chairman), Princeton (also as Dean), UCLA, and as visitor at Columbia and Hawaii.

N. John Hall is Distinguished Professor of English at Bronx Community College and the Graduate School, City University of New York. His publications include *Trollope: A Biography, The Letters of Anthony Trollope, The Trollope Critics,* and *Trollope and his Illustrators.* He is general editor of the thirty-six-title Arno Press *Selected Works of*

Anthony Trollope and of various editions of Trollope for Bantam, Oxford World's Classics, and Everyman Library. He has also brought out expanded editions of Max Beerbohm's *Zuleika Dobson, Rossetti and his Circle,* and *A Christmas Garland* for Yale University Press.

John Halperin is the author of two critically acclaimed biographies, *Gissing: A Life in Books* and *The Life of Jane Austen,* of two volumes of biographical essays, *Novelists in their Youth,* and *Eminent Georgians,* of *C.P. Snow: An Oral Biography,* and of an influential study of Trollope's politics. A Fellow of the Royal Society of Literature and the recipient of two Guggenheim fellowships, he is Centennial Professor of English at Vanderbilt University.

Eric Jacobs was born and brought up in Glasgow, and graduated in English from Oxford University. For thirty years a Fleet Street journalist, principally with *The Sunday Times,* he has written or co-written five books on social and political issues. His book on Kingsley Amis is his first biography.

Justin Kaplan is the author of *Mr Clemens and Mark Twain* (for which he won the Pulitzer Prize in Biography and the National Book Award in Arts and Letters), *Lincoln Steffens: A Biography,* and *Walt Whitman: A Life* (also a National Book Award winner). He served as General Editor of the 16th Edition of *Bartlett's Familiar Quotations.*

Margaret Lewis is the author of *Ngaio Marsh: A Life* and *Edith Pargeter: Ellis Peters.* Lewis was born in Northern Ireland and grew up in Western Canada. She now lives in Newcastle upon Tyne, where she works in the Public Relations Department of Newcastle University. She is an active member of the Crime Writers' Association.

Elizabeth Longford is best known for her prize-winning work *Queen Victoria: Born to Succeed,* and the two-volume life of Wellington, *Years of the Sword* and *Pillar of State.* Her thoughts on the years she spent among the 'best and the brightest' of English society have been published in her 'memoirs', *The Pebbled Shore.*

Diane Wood Middlebrook is a professional writer and Professor of English at Stanford University. Her biography of the poet Anne Sexton spent eight weeks as a *New York Times* Best Seller after publication in 1991 and was a finalist for the National Book Award. She is currently working on the biography of jazz musician Billy Tipton, a woman who lived a fifty-year professional and personal life masquerading as a man.

Andrew Motion has been the recipient of the John Llewellyn Rhys Prize, the Somerset Maugham Award, and the Dylan Thomas Award. His publications include seven collections of poetry, critical studies of Philip Larkin and Edward Thomas, and two biographies, *The Lamberts* and *Philip Larkin: A Writer's Life*. Currently Professor of Creative Writing at the University of East Anglia, he is writing a biography of John Keats.

Katherine Ramsland is a professor of Philosophy at Rutgers University and holds a master's degree in clinical psychology. She writes both fiction and nonfiction and her books include *Prism of the Night: A Biography of Anne Rice, The Vampire Companion, The Witches' Companion, The Anne Rice Trivia Book, The Roquelaure Reader, The Art of Learning,* and *Engaging the Immediate: Applying Kierkegaard's Indirect Communication to Psychotherapy.*

Dale Salwak is professor of English at Southern California's Citrus College. He was educated at Purdue University and then the University of Southern California under a National Defense Education Act competitive fellowship program. In 1985 he was awarded a National Endowment for the Humanities grant. In 1987 Purdue University awarded him its Distinguished Alumni Award. His publications include *The Wonders of Solitude* (New World Library), and studies of Kingsley Amis, John Braine, A.J. Cronin, Philip Larkin, Barbara Pym, Carl Sandburg, Anne Tyler, and John Wain. He is now completing a literary study of the English Bible.

Kenneth Silverman has taught American literature at New York University for thirty years, and is co-director of the NYU Biography Seminar. In addition to the biographies mentioned in this essay (*The Life and Times of Cotton Mather, Edgar A. Poe: Mournful and Never-ending Remembrance,* and *Houdini!!!*), his books include *Timothy Dwight* and *A Cultural History of the American Revolution.* He has received an Edgar Award from the Mystery Writers of America, the Bancroft Prize for American History, and the Pulitzer Prize in Biography.

Natasha Spender (Natasha Litvin) is known for her work as a concert pianist and as a cognitive psychologist of music. She is at present working on memoirs.

Martin Stannard is Professor of Modern English Literature at the University of Leicester. He is the editor of *Evelyn Waugh: The Critical Heritage* and author of *Evelyn Waugh: The Early Years, 1903–1939* and *Evelyn Waugh: No Abiding City, 1939–1966* (American edition, *The Later Years*). His Norton Critical Edition of Ford Madox Ford's *The Good Soldier* has just been published and he is currently at work on the authorized biography of Muriel Spark.

Linda Wagner-Martin, Hanes Professor of English and Comparative Literature at the University of North Carolina, Chapel Hill, has recently published *Telling Women's Lives: The New Biography* and a family biography of Gertrude Stein and her siblings (*'Favored Strangers': Gertrude Stein and Her Family*). Besides the Plath biography, Wagner-Martin has written or edited more than thirty-five books on modern American authors. With Cathy Davidson, she has recently co-edited *The Oxford Companion to Women's Writing in the United States* and its companion anthology, *The Oxford Book of Women's Writing*.

1

A Culture of Biography*

JUSTIN KAPLAN

Woody and Mia, Charles, Camilla, and Diana (also known as Squidgy), Joey and Amy, O.J. and Nicole, Hillary and Bill, John and Lorena, Oprah and Roseanne, Tonya and Nancy; a list like this molts and grows every fifteen minutes. We enjoy a non-stop transitory first-name intimacy with a great deal of secondhand experience. We blur the difference between news, entertainment, scandal, and trivia. The broadsheet *New York Times* and the tabloid *Weekly World News* often serve up the same dish, although the presentation differs. Issues and ideas don't shape daily discourse – celebrity, personality, and anec- dote do. We've become a culture of biography.

Biography as we know it is largely an Anglo-American phenome- non. Other societies draw a stricter line than we do between public and private arenas, between the work and the life. They don't share our obsession with childhood and adolescence, 'creativity' and 'identity', the quirkiness and singularities of private lives. We assume we have a right to know everything about other people. This includes knowing what they 'do' in bed – with whom and with what – even though it can be argued that this may have only a strained connection with what they do out in the world. By current standards, biographies without voyeuristic, erotic thrills are like ballpark hot-dogs without mustard. For a society that feeds on packaged information and instan- taneous celebrity, the notion of privacy is almost as anachronistic as the buttonhook. Although legally moot, the distinction between public figures who are fair game for comment and private people who think they shouldn't be – between the individual's 'right to privacy' and the public's 'need' to know – has been blurring for centuries. 'The business of the biographer,' said Samuel Johnson, 'is to lead the

*This essay is adapted from the John Hersey Memorial Lecture at the 1994 Key West Literary Seminar on biography and autobiography.

1

thoughts into domestic privacies, and display the minute details of daily life.'[1] Coleridge complained about an 'Age of Personality . . . of literary and political gossiping, when the meanest insects are worshipped with a sort of Egyptian superstition.'[2]

It's become a commonplace to speak of a 'golden age' of English-language biography that had its beginnings with Johnson and James Boswell in the eighteenth century, produced notable work in the nineteenth (J.G. Lockhart's *Walter Scott* and J.A. Froude's *Thomas Carlyle*, for example), and was reinvigorated in the twentieth by Lytton Strachey, who celebrated biography as 'the most delicate and humane of all the branches of the art of writing.'[3] By now biography has become our version of folk epic, a tribal exercise in which we tell and interpret the stories of lives that seem to hold some degree of at least passing fascination. The curiosity biography satisfies is as natural and self-justified as breathing.

'All the lonely people – where do they all come from?' We inhabit a culture of loneliness and disengagement, of eroded loyalties and divided communities. But at the same time, and largely through the instrumentality of television, we've come to devalue solitude, mistaking it for loneliness, and have lost whatever ability we once had to endure, respect, and profit from it. Whatever its excesses and limitations, biography is an antidote for loneliness and a restorative of solitude. It shapes the way we frame experience through narrative and character, the way we look at history and other people.

Perhaps it's a reaction against what is often cited as the glumness, grotesquerie, and psychic isolationism of much serious contemporary fiction. But biography at its best emulates – perhaps anachronistically – the imaginative world of the great classic novels: *Madame Bovary, Vanity Fair, David Copperfield, War and Peace, Huckleberry Finn, Remembrance of Things Past.* I'm thinking of biographies like Strachey's *Queen Victoria,* Henri Troyat's *Tolstoy,* Robert Caro's *The Power Broker,* the life of New York City's masterbuilder, Robert Moses. We share in the lives of their protagonists, something we rarely do when we read today's novels and short stories. Good biography exercises what C. Wright Mills called 'the sociological imagination';[4] it explores the intersection of history, society, and individual experience. It renders individual character in the round, tells a generously contexted story that has a beginning, middle, and end, and may even suggest a degree of social continuity and personal responsibility. And good biography does this without moralizing – and to the extent that it judges, it does so, as Walt Whitman said of poetry, 'not as the judge judges but as the sun falling around a helpless thing.'[5]

Along with a torrent of new and reprinted biography published each year there's been a remarkable proliferation of books, lectures, symposia, academic conferences, essays, and literary journals *about* biography – its theory, practice, history, and generic self-awareness. The books are titled *Telling Lives*, *Extraordinary Lives*, *Shaping Lives*, *Writing Lives*, and similar variations on the theme. Strachey madè fun of fat two-volume biographies, but he himself is the subject of a two-volume 1229-page biography; James Boswell, of a wall of Boswelliana. 'Life Likenesses: The Seductions of Biography,' a 1993 conference at Harvard, offered topics like 'Postmodern Biography as Witness to History' and 'Celebrity and Bisexuality.' ('There's almost an eroticism about biography,' said one panelist. 'We want to know the real story' [*Boston Globe*, 17 October 1993].) Such concentrated focus on the genre is a fairly recent development in our culture of biography. I wonder if the theory and practice, the function and future, of fiction or poetry or history are getting anywhere near the same share of attention. I wonder, too, whether such subtilizing refinement and self-consciousness in theory (combined, in practice, with more sensationalism and less and less seriousness) may not be signs that biography is entering its 'silver age'.

At the low end of the biography status scale are *People* magazine, the supermarket tabloids, and television programs like *Hard Copy*, *Inside Edition*, and *A Current Affair* – all in all, an inexhaustible slop bucket of inside stories about the rich, famous, and dysfunctional. Biographies of movie and rock stars and athletes are a little higher on the scale. Then come the collected works of Kitty Kelley, the Saddam Hussein of privacy invasion. Symptomatic of the impacted condition of biography, a writer named George Carpozzi, Jr has even written Ms Kelley's biography and titled it *Poison Pen* (he's also 'done' Jacqueline Kennedy, Gary Cooper, and John Wayne). There wasn't much left of Nancy Reagan after Ms Kelley finished with her (in *Nancy Reagan: The Unauthorized Biography*) except a mound of beak and feathers. I almost admire Ms Kelley for her scouring thoroughness and her eye for unsavory detail. What she gives us by way of biography is pretty much what the culture asks for and deserves. Her critics claim that her books are essentially drive-by shootings, but they're biographies all the same, just as novels by Danielle Steel and Barbara Taylor Bradford are novels no matter what Flaubert or Virginia Woolf might think.

David McCullough's thoroughly engrossing account of Harry Truman figured conspicuously in the 1992 presidential campaign. Both candidates and both parties cited McCullough's book for their purposes. David Brock's *The Real Anita Hill: The Untold Story* also made news. A reviewer in *The Nation* (28 June 1993) argued that it reflected 'a journalistic standard so low that no reputable publishing house should have touched it.' For quite a while, however, *The Real Anita Hill* rode high on the best-seller lists. In an op-ed piece in the *New York Times* (3 December 1992), the surviving children of Joseph and Rose Kennedy denounced Nigel Hamilton's *JFK: Reckless Youth* as 'a grotesque portrait of our parents.' They said their 'earliest . . . memories [were] of exchanging goodnight kisses with Mother and Dad every night.' Six months later, as the *New York Times* (26 June 1993) reported, the Kennedy children were apparently 'gearing up' to go after Joe McGinniss for his biography of Senator Edward M. Kennedy, *The Last Brother*, which was then about to be published. As it turned out, there was no need for the Kennedys to do anything about this book, an innovative subgenre of biography that McGinniss eventually identified as a 'rumination.' The critical response to *The Last Brother* suggests that McGinniss not only shot himself in the foot but followed the Senator's example and drove off the bridge. Its sole interest, said one reviewer in *The New York Times Book Review* (22 August 1993), lay in the questions it inadvertently raised about 'the wiles of the publishing industry' and the nature of 'America's voyeuristic marketplace.' The resulting furor and ethical breast-beating may have had to do less with the book itself than with our own alarm about the addictiveness of biography and the extent to which it rules our lives.

As for 'literary biographies' that generate news beyond the book pages, recall Ian Hamilton's aborted work on J.D. Salinger. To block its publication, Salinger, a celebrated recluse who hadn't submitted to an interview in years, came out of hiding in Cornish, New Hampshire, and, under vigorous questioning, testified at length in a New York lawyer's office. His remarkably revealing deposition went public immediately and at considerable cost to his privacy but he prevailed: Hamilton, who had innocently (to take the most tolerant view) set out to write a literary biography called *J.D. Salinger: A Life*, had to retreat to the legal hideyhole of a barebones account published under the title, *The Search for J.D. Salinger*. This was a 'metabiography': its subject was not Salinger but, in the tradition of A.J.A. Symons' brilliant *Quest for Corvo*, the problems involved in writing about Salinger.

The hot center of Diane Middlebrook's biography of the poet Anne Sexton was not the poetry but transcripts of hours and hours of Sexton's sessions with one of her psychoanalysts. This caused an uproar over medical and literary ethics, confidentiality, and the privacy of the dead as well as the living. The same degree of inflamed public attention has also been bestowed less on the work than on the life and suicide of Sylvia Plath, the subject of about half a dozen biographies and Janet Malcolm's adroitly self-serving account, 'Annals of Biography: The Silent Woman' in *The New Yorker* (23 and 30 August 1993). Ms Malcolm analyzed the traffic between Plath's biographers, taken singly and as a group; Plath's husband and sister-in-law, who are the custodians of her posthumous reputation and literary estate; and Malcolm herself, who plunges into a slough of contention and comes out of it washed whiter than snow. Her own roles as prosecutor, judge, and jury excepted, she sees this long-running imbroglio as an allegory of 'subjects' (and readers) victimized by a corrupt narrative convention. Biography, she writes, 'is the medium through which the remaining secrets of the famous dead are taken from them and dumped out in full view of the world. The biographer at work, indeed, is like the professional burglar, breaking into a house, rifling through certain drawers that he has good reason to think contain the jewelry and the money, and triumphantly bearing this away.'

The thrust and imagery of Malcolm's fulmination inevitably call up Henry James's *The Aspern Papers*. Sly and manipulative, but rather thick all the same, the narrator (or anti-hero, or even villain) of this brimstone-and-hellfire fiction about biography lies his way into the Venetian palazzo of an aged woman. He wants what she's got: the private papers of her one-time lover, a famous dead author named Jeffrey Aspern. He plays on the old woman's penury and on the vulnerability of her 'plain, dingy, elderly' niece, whom he leads to believe that after her aunt's death he may marry for her dowry – the Aspern papers. In one of the several climaxes of this ferocious fable, the old woman discovers the biographer about to break into her secretary. 'I never shall forget', he says, 'the tone in which . . . she hissed out passionately, furiously: "Ah, you publishing scoundrel!"' The old woman dies; the niece burns the papers; the narrator's 'chagrin' at their loss is 'almost intolerable.'

Resentment of 'publishing scoundrels' was nothing new when Henry James published his story. The 'golden age of biography' had added a new terror to death: 'the journeymen of letters' (Strachey's phrase) who followed the physician, clergyman, and undertaker into the house of lamentation. 'Biographies are murder,' said Henry Adams. 'They belittle the victim and the assassin equally.'[6] He regarded his masterful autobiography, *The Education of Henry Adams*, as 'a shield of protection in the grave', a preemptive move in which he 'took his life' in his own way in order to prevent biographers from taking it in theirs. (An unavailing tactic, as it turned out: Henry Adams dead is a thriving industry for American biographers and scholars.) In the same hope of fending off biographers, Charles Dickens made a bonfire of his private papers and invited his children to roast potatoes and onions in the embers. Walt Whitman, Henry James, and other writers followed Dickens's example to such an extent that our view of the landscape of nineteenth-century literature is partially obscured by the smoke rising from these archival pyres, which is not to say that the biographers have been deterred from doing their work.

Closer to our time, the writer Germaine Greer has somewhere described biography as 'rape . . . an unpardonable crime against selfhood.' Others say that biography is voyeuristic, invasionary, exploitative, a wild-goose chase: its methods are obsolete, its premises shaky, its promises of unmediated reporting altogether fraudulent, and its end product just a pile of paper and a collection of gossip. Biography, says Roland Barthes, is 'a novel that dare not speak its name'.[7] Julian Barnes, author of *Flaubert's Parrot*, says biography can be compared to a net – 'a collection of holes tied together with strings,'[8] those holes containing half-truths, untruths, evasions, and incongruities. The reality of the life slips away like a greased piglet, a flown bird. The book the author creates, Proust wrote in *Contre Saint-Beuve*, 'is the product of a different *self* from the self we manifest in our habits, in our social life, in our vices. . . . What one bestows on private life . . . is the product of a quite superficial self, not of the innermost self which one can only recover by putting aside the world and the self that frequents the world.'[9]

Still others decry the elitism and phallocentrism of conventional biography, its implicit gospel of success, devaluation of autonomous 'texts', and market-driven tendency to produce narratives that highlight fetishism, kinkiness, addiction, alcoholism, incest, violence, abuse, and suicide. *Pathography* – a term introduced by Sigmund Freud in his study of Leonardo da Vinci and recently recycled by Joyce Carol

Oates – denotes life-accounts that make you wonder how their subjects managed to get out of bed in the morning, much less write novels or poems, paint pictures, compose music, become leaders, make money, or do any other part of the world's work. Going public with pain is now a literary convention as well as a social imperative, and one could easily infer an entire society of victims, co-dependents, and candidates for a universal twelve-step program.

The biographer might be described as a hermit crab inhabiting the shell of another's life or as a jockey who takes credit for his horse's speed and mettle. The 'how' – the writer's skill – became at least as important as the 'who' – the writer's subject – when biographers began to think of themselves not as chroniclers or post-mortem amanuenses but as shapers and participants, agonistic heroes and joint-tenants in posthumous lives. Is the biographer a grave-robber? A harmless fantasist? 'Sometimes when we think that we are rediscovering the mighty dead', the philosopher Richard Rorty says in *The New Republic* (18 June 1989), 'we are just inventing imaginary playmates.' 'What are you really like?' Virginia Woolf asked Vita Sackville-West, her model for *Orlando*. 'Do you exist? Have I made you up?'[10]

Consider the fable of biography one might extract from an elaborate ruse the British devised in the Second World War and codenamed 'Operation Mincemeat.'[11] They invented a complete identity and life history for a corpse they then launched from a submarine in the Mediterranean. Uniformed and documented as Major W. Martin of the Royal Marines, the corpse carried authentic-sounding but totally false documents about Allied invasion plans along with dog tags, love letters, family letters, overdraft notices, legal papers, tailor's bills, theater tickets, fiancée photo, and the like: the raw materials of biography and precisely the sort of 'corroborative detail' that, as Pooh-Bah says in *The Mikado*, gives 'artistic verisimilitude to an otherwise bald and unconvincing narrative.' A Spanish fisherman turned 'Major Martin' over to the Germans, who swallowed 'Mincemeat' whole and shifted their defensive forces to the wrong landing site. 'The Man Who Never Was' had gone to war, carried out his mission of duping the enemy, and lies in a Spanish cemetery under a headstone with the Horatian inscription, *Dulce et decorum est pro patria mori* ('It is sweet and honorable to die for one's country'). Some biographical launchings and reanimations – for example, Carl Sandburg's *Abraham Lincoln* – have had comparable histories. Edmund Wilson called Sandburg's six-volume work of mythopoesis 'the cruellest thing that has happened to Lincoln since he was shot by Booth.'

One consequence of the saturating presence of biography is an invasion of the body snatchers. It's getting tougher every day to find what is commonly but unfeelingly called a 'subject,' especially one not 'taken' or 'done,' at least recently. Some writers get in on the ground floor with a person still kicking, but there are problems here: control, perspective, and especially closure, deathbed and interment scenes being among the ornaments of traditional biography. Better would be someone in the early stages of historical rigor mortis, with the ghost still on the premises, and furnished with private papers and compliant heirs. In any case, to write biography you need oxlike endurance, resignation to the swift passing of time without much to show for it, and the capacity to feed on your own blood when other sources run dry. You're committing a serious act of literature, that is, if you take biography as seriously as it deserves to be taken. Lives as lived don't have the shape of art, but lives as *written* ought at least to acknowledge strivings in that direction. The work doesn't get any easier as you go along from book to book. You may have acquired narrative and stylistic skills, a little bit of confidence, and some understanding of what makes people and biographies tick, but at the same time your standards go up and you demand more and more of yourself. Above all, between you and the person you write about there has to be an intimate link, not necessarily one of affection or sympathy – Adolf Hitler is an endlessly fascinating subject, as is Richard Nixon – but one of passionate, sustainable interest. In my experience, finding this link is almost as rare as seeing the legendary green flash at sundown.

I was lucky the first time. A close friend, then editor-in-chief at Pocket Books, said over a long lunch one day, 'Why don't you write a biography of Mark Twain?' and I answered, 'I'll do it.' It was an electrifying idea, the real right thing at the right time. I resigned a perfectly good editorial job in New York and spent the next seven years with Mark Twain. A good part of that time was wasted in pure fright: I had never written a full-length book before, much less a biography of someone as masterful, iconic, and original as Mark Twain. To sustain me I had the encouragement of my wife, the novelist Anne Bernays, and several exemplars, among them Lytton Strachey, for his stylistic brilliance; Samuel Johnson, for the existential textures of his life of Richard Savage; Margaret Leach (*Reveille in Washington*) and Cecil Woodham-Smith (*The Reason Why*), for their interweaving of documentary and biography; Geoffrey Scott, for the concision and elegance of his *Portrait of Zelide;* and Erik Erikson (*Childhood and Society,*

Young Man Luther), for liberating us from Sigmund Freud's cramping theology (as it seemed) of foreordination. And one fine day I realized that I was indeed able to write the sort of biography that I would have wanted to publish if I had still been an editor. After the reviews came out, and then the National Book Award and the Pulitzer Prize, someone I barely knew stopped me on the street and said, 'That's all very well, but what are you going to do for an encore?' It's a question that never goes away.

I went on to write a biography of Lincoln Steffens, the grandfather of muckraking and investigative journalism; a second book about Mark Twain; and then a biography of Walt Whitman, an old interest of mine. But it took me several years to figure out how I wanted to tell Whitman's story, and this was: not to begin with an infant born in the first administration of President James Monroe but with an aged man, an invalid, living in a raddled house in Camden, New Jersey, and looking back over the well-travelled roads that had led to the writing and defense of *Leaves of Grass*.

I am also the author of many unwritten books. One of them was a biography of Ulysses Grant, general-in-chief of the Union armies, global hero, and two-term president of the United States, in his earlier life a reluctant soldier, a business failure, and a drunk. Here was the sort of archetypal figure I had been looking for: a shabby firewood peddler divinely endowed with strength and a charisma so powerful that General William Tecumseh Sherman, a nonbeliever, said he fought under Grant with 'the faith a Christian has in his Savior.' But after about a year of living with Grant I began to develop such a long list of reluctances (having to do with refighting the Civil War and detailing his disastrous presidencies, his bankruptcy, and his slow death of throat cancer) that I was left with an idea for what could only be a tiny book about Ulysses Grant and his rapport with horses. Finally, after reviewing for the *New Republic* a spirited and thoroughgoing new biography of Grant by William S. McFeely, I decided we wouldn't be needing another biography of Grant in this generation anyhow.

Eventually the name of Charlie Chaplin replaced Grant's on my Simon & Schuster contract. That's another story altogether, although it doesn't end any better. The year and more I spent on Chaplin had its redeeming adventures. Oona, his widow, forthcoming one moment, inaccessible the next, was as changeable as the drunk millionaire in *City Lights*. I saw her in New York and in Vevey, Switzerland, where I spent a couple of weeks rummaging through Charlie's papers and scripts, his contracts and income tax returns, which were stored in one of the dungeons of his stone manor house. The adjacent dungeon, a temperature-and-humidity-controlled vault, housed Chaplin's films and Oona's fur coats. As I worked down there, knowing that on the upper floors were the elusive chatelaine and her silent servitors, I thought of the remote castle in Ann Radcliffe's *Mysteries of Udolpho* and began to develop a serious case of the creeps. In the end I gave up on Charlie, too, for several compelling reasons.

One is that so much movie history, autobiography, memoir, and the like is pure moonshine, making it virtually impossible to tell lies from the truth. 'The tragedy of film history,' the actress Louise Brooks wrote, 'is that it is fabricated, falsified by the very people who make film history,'[12] and those people included Chaplin, the author of several autobiographies.

Chaplin was a genius in his line, but everything brilliant and charming and original about him appears to have gone into his movies, which are gestural, speak for themselves, and so don't need the nudging of a biographer. What was left over wasn't sufficiently compelling. Even his steamy private life – his affairs and divorces, his involvements with underage women, and a paternity suit – had a certain repetitious quality. In an important sense, this man never grew beyond the age of fourteen, no matter how old and famous he got to be. In two or three early chapters I could have demonstrated – at least to my own satisfaction – that his traumatic boyhood (his drunk father and lunatic mother, his time in the orphan asylum and begging in the streets) was not only formative but supplied the text and subtext for practically every one of his movies. Having made that point, I realized that this was going to be a biography that told the same story of need and restitution over and over again. That wasn't the kind of book I wanted to write or read. So it was, 'Good-bye Charlie.'

Passing over in charitable silence my investigations of Gertrude Stein, Willa Cather, Stephen Crane, Edgar Allan Poe, and a few others, I come to what I still consider to have been an ideal prospect for biography. This was Irving Berlin, whose daughters offered me access to his papers, their cooperation, and the pledge of a hands-off policy as far as control or approval of the final product was concerned. Berlin had transformed American entertainment culture and made his name synonymous with American music. This immigrant Jew took over Christmas and Easter in his songs and made 'God Bless America' a national anthem. He couldn't write or read scores but picked out hundreds of great tunes on his keyboard and had the musical equivalent of a stenographer take them down. English was not his first language, but he was a brilliant lyricist in English. And there was great personal and public drama in this story as well: Berlin's secret courtship of a Roman Catholic society beauty, the furor over their elopement and marriage, the unremitting enmity of his rich father-in-law. I had the impression that Irving Berlin had something of a rebarbative and recessive nature, but I felt for him, and with him, and believed that empathy if not love would conquer all things.

As it turned out, two of the daughters drew back when I asked for an important cycle of letters and messages their parents had exchanged during their courtship – these things were too private, too sacred, I was told, even for the most indirect background use in a biography, and if I were even to see these papers I was not to acknowledge it. I realized that if I accepted these (and some other) restrictions I would probably have to spend years of wheedling and negotiating to get whatever else I needed to see. I also realized that even the most kindly disposed biographer enters an adversarial situation when family feelings about adored parents are involved, but all the same I took this withdrawal of trust as an affront to my integrity. The venture had been irreparably compromised, and I bowed out. As Henry James's narrator would say, my 'chagrin' over the loss of this unwritten book was 'almost intolerable.' My last working note on the Irving Berlin project reads: 'Bring up violin music. Fade to blackout and curtain.'

2

Biography – The Scarlet Experiment

ANTONY ALPERS

Biographies fall roughly into three kinds (and many more, I am sure), depending on the author's distance from his human subject in space and time. Setting aside all books on living persons, there is first the biography written fairly soon after the subject's death by someone who knew him, and who perhaps has access to personal papers. This is not the commonest kind, but I put it first because it enjoys advantages that can never be repeated. I shall call it the personal biography; the author once saw Shelley plain, and there is no substitute for that. But perhaps he cannot wait for the death of the daughter, or for certain letters to become available. Whether 'authorized' or not, he needs to write the book and publish it. For every advantage he enjoys, this author may suffer frustrations too, and only exceptional gifts and circumstances, such as those of Boswell, can transcend the difficulties.

Then comes the class which, using shorthand, I shall call the proximate or reported biography. The author may not have known his subject personally (his or hers, we must nowadays say, and the gain is immense), but he either possesses, or is equipped to acquire, a thorough understanding of the human subject's background and sphere of activities – perhaps in public action, or in science, or one of the arts. If he was not actually there, he is near enough in time to go there; and working soon enough, with the necessary tact and gifts – perhaps a touch of the detective, or some historical training to help him – this author can turn his unattachment to account and produce biography of a superior sort. George Painter, Enid Starkie, Michael Holroyd come to mind among practitioners in the literary field. Mention of the last of course brings Lytton Strachey into view, a writer who changed biography in our century though employing hardly any of the advantages so far mentioned. But the uses of irony and 'brilliance' in biography are a topic apart. They can displace for a time, but not replace, what the craft demands.

Using shorthand again, I shall call my third category the historical biography. The writer in this class works after the dust has settled – and dust in the eyes there is, for the previous two. He or she never once saw Shelley plain (and sometimes wakes in the night wishing that were possible – *just once*). But 'plainer' is not impossible, perhaps? This biographer works from books and documents, unburdened by the drudgeries (and wasted journeys for fruitless interviews) endured by the other two kinds; untainted also by that touch of the low detective. Kings and queens, revolutionaries and other great personages, including artists, may be his or her material, in which case librarians and earlier scholars (bless them all for their selfless labors) have long since made accessible a vast array of printed facts and sources, assembling collections, compiling bibliographies, and sorting out that costliest, most labor-intensive treasure, the simple chronology, without which cause-and-effect deductions can turn to nonsense. Through the magic of print their corporate labors can be scanned in minutes. One can even take a bibliography to bed. The other two writers had to do their work 'too soon,' which is to say not late enough. The historical biographer is more fortunate, for with the greatest and most enduring human subjects there is no such thing as 'too late'. Could anyone say 'too late' of Walter Jackson Bate's magnificent work on Samuel Johnson?

Those are the three main categories, and of course some intervening kinds will come to mind (the historical biographer given privileged late access to 'the papers' may constitute a separate class). But broadly speaking, the biographer cannot step outside the class that has been ordained for him by time. He is condemned to know moments of exasperated envy for practitioners in either or both of the other two classes. He owns no time machine, and as a rule receives no second chance.

It so happens that within one third of a century I have had the experience of working to completion in the second two classes of biography – the reported and the historical – on the self-same human subject. I did receive a second chance, and the experience seems worth reporting on. If not unique, it must be most unusual, since it can only occur where a young biographer writes of a subject who died young, and can later return to the task when the subject's friends have died.

Some thirty years ago, I wrote a biography of my compatriot Katherine Mansfield, beginning it in New Zealand and completing it in England, on the pattern of her own short life. It was a young man's book: I was twenty-seven when I began it, and still twenty-seven when I finished it four years later, or so I think when forced to look at it; and at the time of publication Katherine Mansfield (1888–1923) would only have been in her sixties. Thus many of her contemporaries and friends were still alive – not Lawrence though, nor Virginia Woolf, nor Ottoline Morrell, nor A.R. Orage. In writing the book I had the help of both of K.M.'s husbands, two of her sisters, the adoring Ida Baker whom she once referred to as her 'wife,' and several others who had been intimate friends at one time or another. But in publishing it I also had to think of them, since all but one of my informants lived to read it. Because K.M. had died when I was three it was not a personal biography, class one; it was one of the reported kind, class two. Of letters and papers I had access to very little, so it was not historical either. At the time I naïvely thought that I was working 'late enough,' since my subject had been dead for thirty years, but in fact the time for distancing must be measured from the birth, not from the death.

In 1948 and 1949 I visited people in England for whom Katherine was still a vivid presence in the room (in one case she had sat there too, at the downstairs kitchen table of S.S. Koteliansky's house in St John's Wood), and they were kind, and disposed to help me; but when I asked about letters they used polite evasions, suppressing the thought that was in their minds: 'Jack Murry is still alive.' I was in touch with him, of course; for Middleton Murry was the executor, and owner of the rights, and he was then working on a new edition of the *Journal*, and of all the letters too (or, so he thought). For access to the letters and papers which he owned, I did not even ask. But to the writing of that book I would like to return after speaking of my second attempt.

When a dozen years had passed, in the 1960s, the first biography went out of print; and then a great change came over my life. Partly on the strength of the book, I was invited in 1966 by Dr George Whalley to join the Department of English at Queen's University, in Kingston, Ontario. Four years later it was he who suggested that I might 'revise' it, in the light of new material. I would be eligible for research funds, and for sabbatical leave – unaccustomed privileges for me.

I set to work, and within a year or so I began to understand what had really happened. Because of deaths in the previous fifteen years, all the 'papers,' or nearly all, had become available, and very great quantities had crossed the Atlantic to North America; in Texas, the inward correspondence of Lady Ottoline Morrell, packed with references to Mansfield and Murry at Garsington; in the Berg Collection of the New York Public Library, the diary and other papers of Virginia Woolf, not then published, and papers of Edward Marsh, who was part of the story too; in the British Museum, those of Koteliansky (once withheld from me) and of Katherine Mansfield's cousin 'Elizabeth,' of the *German Garden;* in Hamilton, Ontario, the archives of Bertrand Russell, who in 1916 made a pass at Katherine Mansfield (I think that describes it) while also having an affair with Lady Constance Malleson and still addressing Ottoline Morrell as 'My Darling' in every letter now in Texas (also sending descriptions of K.M. to both of them). Finally, and very important: in New Zealand there now were all the notebooks, manuscripts, and letters from K.M. herself which Murry had owned in 1950, but which I had not then seen. There were even people still living, in their eighties, who could help me, and one man in his nineties: Katherine's first husband, George Bowden, whom she had deserted for a young violinist whose letters from her, unknown to me as yet, were also in Ontario.

What had really happened, then, was this. I had written one biography 'too soon,' with access to many personal impressions from my subject's intimate friends, but with dust in my eyes as well; in some sense a personal biography, class one, but really a reported biography, class two. And now, with access to hoards of letters and papers including her own (and research funds enabling me to get to them, because that is a recognized part of the academic life in North America) I was to come at the subject again, in class three. I was to have a second chance.

Was it 'easier,' because I had done it before and therefore knew the story? It was not. It was very much harder, and it took more than twice as long. The 'story' was in fact a different one, at least to me. It was a question partly of dust in the eyes the first time round (not only the image of Murry's idealized, 'perfect' Katherine to be expunged, but also Ida Baker's much less innocent creation of a different perfect Katherine); and partly of mastering all that fresh material on a vastly greater scale. In 1950 my files and notes and books could all be got into a Rinso carton, which could be slid under a bed, such was life in those days. The equivalent materials for the second biography, collected with the help of Queen's University, the Canada Council, the Xerox Corporation, modern filing equipment, and uncounted airlines, amounted in simple shelf-length to twenty times as much.

This enormous increase had three independent causes, which I recapitulate: deaths or impoverishment of owners (and the value in dollars of literary papers from that period); research facilities normal to the academic world into which I had been invited (not quite so normal now); and the technological advance of photocopying, the effect of which on literary researches is a fascinating topic I should really not embark on. Given photocopies, you can visit that library again and again without supporting the airlines; you can punch holes in Xerox copies, put them in binders, and move them about as chronology emerges; you can make notes on them, for dating and other purposes; you can even take them to bed, in book form. Next morning while shaving the solution suddenly appears, as if from nowhere. At the guarded tables of research libraries, in my experience, no solutions ever appear – though they might if I did my shaving there.

I am nearly ready to compare the two experiences of biography, and perhaps to echo Mr Chadband's 'What is terewth?' But it is not every reader who already knows what Katherine Mansfield did in her very short life, or why, or how. Born Kathleen Mansfield Beauchamp in Wellington in 1888, she was the third child – the third *daughter*, and this was her first offence – of an ambitious Colonial businessman who very much wanted a son. In a prosperous family, she became in some sense a rejected child.

At the age of nine she wrote and published her first short story, in the school magazine, and announced that she was 'going to be a writer,' possibly because her father's first cousin had just then published the best-seller *Elizabeth and her German Garden*. She was then a pudgy, moody, difficult girl, a little overweight. At fourteen, looking quite different, she was taken with her sisters to Queen's College, in Harley Street, where Walter Ripmann introduced her to the 'decadents' and to Oscar Wilde. In her writing of the time there is a noticeable death-wish theme. Taken back to Wellington she loathed the place, kicked over the traces, and made her father agree to her going alone to London in 1908 with £100 a year from him. Her driving ambition then was to write short stories of a kind that did not then exist, with a strong conception of 'form' (she used the word, having heard it from Walter Ripmann I believe). But she also fell in love with a penniless young musician, whose father put his foot down. Inexplicably, she married the much older George Bowden in 1909, left him the same evening, joined the violinist in a touring opera company, became pregnant by him, and then was packed off by her flying-visit Mother to Bavaria – not because she was pregnant (her mother did not know that), but because of her 'unhealthy relationship' with her English school-friend

Ida Baker. The baby miscarried in Worishofen. She wrote there of her feeling that she might die young.

Returning to London in 1910, she began writing stories for A.R. Orage's *New Age*. In 1912 she threw in her lot instead with John Middleton Murry, aged twenty-two, and his magazine called *Rhythm*. They lived together, with Ida Baker often near and always needed. Then Lawrence and Frieda turned up and tossed their lives around. They saw her as a liar, but, as Frieda once said, 'she also knows more about truth than other people and don't let us see too much the *ugly* things.' Katherine meanwhile had tuberculosis, but did not know it yet; she learnt that in 1918, and nearly all of her best writing was done in the five years that remained. With that writing, in pursuit of a certain kind of truth about human behavior and a form in which to express it, she changed the art of the short story in English, but did not quite achieve the fourth book that would have been her best one. She died in 1923, aged thirty-four.

In my new biography, three chapters take her up to the age of nineteen, when she left New Zealand for good, and eighteen more are devoted to the fifteen years that remained – her writing life. (Murry's own biographer, Frank Lea, once told me how he envied me for this compression of the span.) The scheme, except for one chapter on Virginia Woolf, is strictly chronological. But a critical thread is woven in, because in Katherine Mansfield's case the writing and the life are one – shot through with comedy and tragedy. Thus the technical problems are considerable.

Now then: what are the rules for proximate biography, involving 'personal' research? For a start, chronology is everything. Get the facts in order first, and get them right, or ludicrous conclusions may result (and interviews go to waste). This means collecting every trivial fact, in the notes at least, and much detective work; and later, sacrificing precious discoveries. 'Murder your darlings,' said Colette – good advice for the biographer, too. On the subject of gossip, I early formulated one rule for myself: 'Always listen to gossip. The more you hear, the less you will have to use'. (It cancels out.) In 1947 K.M.'s school friend Ruth Herrick, by then the Chief Commissioner of Girl Guides in New Zealand, told me a piece of gossip about an alleged pregnancy which I left out the first time round, not feeling sure of it. Thirty years later, still there in my notes, it turned out to be crucial, and cleared up a mystery, though only because it then linked up with a document.

Depending on temperament, one should probably attempt all possible interviews. Raw from New Zealand, I did not have that temperament. I vividly remember G.E. Moore, whom I used to meet in Cambridge in a purely social way, saying to me once, 'I think *Russell* knew her rather well.'

Tackle Bertrand Russell! I lacked the nerve, and never tried. Yet what could Russell have told me in 1949? With Murry still living, he could hardly have shown me the letters from Katherine which he was just then sorting out (and muddling up the envelopes). He would have had to say, in one of his fine evasions, 'I don't think there is anything more that I can tell you.' Years passed before I handled those letters in Canada, and read what he had written about them in 1949.

Dear, kind Frank Swinnerton, wishing to encourage and help me, suggested I come with him to meet Eliot, but out of respect and shyness I demurred. 'Oh, come on, he's a nice old codger.' Again, what would Eliot, of all people, have been prepared to tell a biographer, scratching in the straw of private lives? In fact, he also knew K.M., but could not have known that one of her comic descriptions, very sympathetic to himself, described an evening spent with him and Robert Graves and Roger Fry in 1917; or that just about that time she gave a reading of *Prufrock* to the assembled guests at Garsington, within a few days of its publication. (Clive Bell recorded that.) There is gossip and gossip, much of it. But in the end it is the documents that count.

Or is it? Is all the truth in them? What does one do with the following exchange of 1949 between Ida Baker (or Lesley Moore) and the woman friend who sponsored our early meetings and tried to bully Lesley into talking: 'Come on Lesley, you're supposed to be one. What is it Lesbians *do*?' 'Well, my darling, I've heard it said – they use *instruments*.' A most revealing remark – revealing innocence, I think. And there can be no substitute for the exact form of words employed. But put it in? No, because every second-rate reviewer would seize upon it, and blow proportion all to hell. It is true that gossip tells, most tellingly. But 'Do not relish it' would be the rule, I now believe; and do not give others the chance to do that thing. Let its tellingness be functional, or refrain.

In 1950 I wrote to the French novelist Francis Carco, with whom K.M. had a brief affair in 1915, actually spending four illicit nights with him in the Zone des Armees where he was a military postman with the rank of corporal. To my surprise he invited me to his flat on the Quai de Bethune, filled with Utrillos. Not reading English, he had never known what K.M. wrote about the episode in her journal, or that Murry had revealed it in print. 'That's annoying' was his comment (not in English). 'I didn't know Jack knew.'

And Murry himself had not known of many things of which he first read in my first biography, for K.M. had used concealment – deceptions too – with him. And so, with Mr Chadbend: 'What is terewth?' Is it what the intimates knew and saw and felt – or what the biographer 'finds out'? Presumably, it must be constructed out of both. But in this regard, not the knowledge of the participants in the story, but the customs of the time in which the teller of it lives, the currently accepted expectations of biography, will play a shaping part. They have greatly changed, between 1950 and 1980. The construct which results may be seen as true, but only for its time. Such a thing as 'definitive biography' does not exist. Because of changes in the view we take, it will always be changing.

There is another change on the way – one caused by new technology. Until about 1960 you had to be a bookworm to write biography; in fact you could be nothing *but* a bookworm, and write biography. From now on you will need to be a tapeworm too – a less attractive beast, I think – and you will be dealing in a different kind of truth. Post-Nixon biography will have different qualities.

Some people talk of oral history. I myself, having made it a rule always to go to an interview equipped with a daunting supply of facts and dates, have found people's memories for facts consistently unreliable, but not their personal impressions of a character, or of feelings, or even of motives. In the end, though, the proximate biographer (class one or class two), must always turn from the spoken word, the revealing gesture, the lifted eyebrow, to that authentic bit of paper with words written on it; he must join class three whenever he can.

But even that may not avail if he lacks a humble attitude towards his own discoveries, and cannot bring himself to follow Colette's advice to novelists. The more he discovers on his own, the greater is his danger in this regard. He is bound to experience a corrupting sense of power at times: 'I seem to know more about this than they did.' K.M.'s unfortunate first husband, George Bowden, once told me that himself, and the fact (for fact it was) had a curious consequence.

When crossing the Atlantic in 1972, knowing that I was to meet him and his wife for the first time (he was then 94; Mrs Bowden was younger), I well remember wondering, as I looked down on the icebergs from 40,000 feet, whether a visit of only four days to their Mediterranean home would be long enough for me to broach with Mrs Bowden the principal question on my mind: 'Have you any idea why Katherine Mansfield married Mr Bowden?' After other travels I arrived, and had been in the house about an hour. Mr Bowden was dozing in the next room, a rug over his knees in his favorite chair. Mrs Bowden, across a table from me, was toying with an ornament, when *she* broached it: 'There's one question I've been wanting to ask you. Have you any idea why Katherine married George?' The whole thing broke up in a laugh, we became good friends, and a little later certain papers were produced. It is the papers, now, that are in the book. Always the papers. The answer to the question itself is still no more than a guess.

Returning to those changes wrought by time in the character of accidental records: it is obvious that the telephone has eliminated all those penny letters that were once so numerous. To Lytton Strachey: 'Thank you. I should love to come to tea at 4:30 on Friday. . . . ' To Bertrand Russell: 'Yes, do let us dine together on the 23rd. . . . ' Those are no more. But the tapeworm of the future will hear what I could not, and would have dearly liked to know: what did Lawrence sound like when he talked? How far did he change his Midlands accent? To what extent did the Colonial Katherine Mansfield sound 'English' after her elocution lessons at Queen's College with the son of the Victorian novelist George Macdonald? Did her voice, her modified 'New Zealand twang' as Murry once called it, grate on the sensibilities of Virginia Woolf and Ottoline Morrell? Future biographers will sometimes have access to this different kind of truth. And what a factor it could be!

Of all K.M.'s precarious relationships, one of the most interesting was that with Virginia Woolf. As woman writers, they were greatly drawn to each other. There was no one else, as Virginia more than once said. But as women, they danced the slow-motion ballet of a couple of wary cats. This is because they both were obliged to hide so much: Virginia, her madness; Katherine, her youthful follies, and the price they had exacted. Two specialists in the secrets of the human heart, brought together by the strong desire to know, and understand: and they could not know each other! In time, with the face-saving movements of two cats, they drew apart. At work on Katherine's side was a loathing of Bloomsbury; on Virginia's, a fascination and recoil from Katherine's appetite for life. The price of that included gonorrhea, which Katherine had for eight years without knowing it (it was in the upper tract), and she only learned the truth at a moment when Virginia was experiencing a desire to know her better, along with a puzzling sense of being avoided. One day as Virginia was leaving the house, Katherine very nearly spoke of it; in fact, she did so in general terms, but then held back. What Virginia's reaction might have been, she dared not learn. Three years later Virginia published *Jacob's Room*, her experiment on the theme that for human beings to know each other really is not possible. Katherine died soon after, not having read it.

Literary biography is an exercise in cutting up the artist to find out how he works – as we used to pull apart our clockwork toys. There is a queer little poem by Emily Dickinson, that other prober into secrets of the human heart, which *sounds* as if it treats this theme. For the last few years I have had it mentally beside me, always accusing, since the life that I was trying to describe came to a terrible end in gushes of blood from Katherine's mouth. Miss Dickinson's caution to the literary biographer:

> Split the Lark – and you'll find the Music –
>   Bulb after Bulb, in Silver rolled –
> Scantily dealt to the Summer Morning
>   Saved for your Ear when Lutes be old
>
> Loose the Flood – you shall find it patent –
>   Gush after Gush, reserved for you –
> Scarlet Experiment! Sceptic Thomas!
>   Now, do you doubt that your Bird was true?

Having committed biography twice I sometimes wonder, after that, whether it ought to be allowed.

3

Those Wonderful Youths and Maidens, My Reviewers

N. JOHN HALL

That lively and shrewd but cold woman [Sartre's grandmother] thought straight but inaccurately. . . . 'They claim the earth goes round. What do they know about it?'

Jean-Paul Sartre, *The Words*

I had not heard of [the reviews in] the Critic *or* Daily News *or* Truth; *– nor if a word be said against me in any newspaper, do I think much of it. I fancy that we authors owe more to critics than any injustice we receive from them. I am sure that if any critic wanted to spite us, he could better do it by holding his tongue than by speaking evil of us.*

Anthony Trollope to Charles Mackay, 19 June 1881

Biography is such a hot topic these days that when you have written one you are frequently asked to give talks or write about the experience of putting together your version of a particular life. As the author of *Trollope: A Biography* (Oxford University Press, 1991), I myself have frequently done so, usually keeping safely to talks given with no view to publication, and in which, accordingly, I could be somewhat off-hand or informal. I have sometimes talked about my more than 20-year involvement with Trollope, about how I got taken up with Trollope in graduate school and just never got away from him (and became that currently unfashionable creature, a 'single-author' specialist). I have discussed how my edition of Trollope's letters occupied a good portion of that time and served as preparation for a biography. I spoke about the two special difficulties of writing Trollope's life, his huge output of nearly 70 books and the uneventful later years. I gave talks on Trollope and women, on Trollope and his reviewers. On occasions I ventured, rather gingerly, on the subject of the great swell of interest in Trollope's life, on the truly phenomenal, perhaps unexampled case of four 'major' (large) biographies in five years: Robert H. Super in late 1988, Richard Mullen in 1990 (Great Britain only), myself in 1991, and Victoria Glendinning in 1992. As biographer number three, I confessed to having only 'looked into' the two that appeared before mine. I won't try to defend that decision here, and will say only that I still believe it was the right one. My idea was that we were all working from the same materials and that in reading other biographies I would be subject to two unhelpful reactions: first, if I saw anything I thought a misuse of the sources I should be annoyed, but certainly wasn't going to spend a line of my own work 'refuting' others; and, second, if I saw anything startlingly insightful or original, I should be annoyed at not having come up with it myself.

For this published essay I have decided to try something that I think fairly novel. I propose to line up against each other excerpts of negative and positive criticisms of my *Trollope*, organizing them under various issues raised by the reviewers. The result should offer graphic evidence of the opposing responses these professional readers have to the same text. I can't recall ever encountering precisely the same stratagem. It's an exercise both humiliating and ego-boosting; it is also a slightly cheeky thing to do, really, but I promise to be (reasonably) fair.

A good place to start is the opening line of the biography: John Powell, quoting that sentence, writes, '"Anthony Trollope was born on 24 April 1815 at 16 Keppel Street, Russell Square, London" is not an auspicious beginning to a major new treatment of one of England's most prolific and popular novelists.'[1]

C.A. Latimer, in *The American Scholar*, also quotes the first line: '[How] reassuring it is to read the opening words, "Anthony Trollope was born on 24 April 1815 at 16 Keppel Street, Russell Square, London." That's how a biography should start.'[2]

Other contrasts may not be as perfectly symmetrical, but they can come pretty close. I shall steer clear of comparisons made among Super, Mullen, and Hall, but here is one between Hall and an early predecessor, James Pope Hennessy. Alan Bold in the *Glasgow Herald*

(31 October 1991) writes, 'In 1972 James Pope Hennessy won the Whitbread Literary Award for a biography acclaimed, by writers as distinguished as C.P. Snow and W.H. Auden, as the best possible portrait of Trollope. Now N. John Hall, editor of Trollope's *Letters*, faults Pope Hennessy's biography as unscholarly: "inadequate in serious ways, including its utter lack of annotation." There is more to biography than identifying sources.'

On the other hand, Donald Lyons, in *The American Spectator*, writes: 'One can take the measure of N. John Hall's calmly comprehensive biography by looking back at James Pope Hennessy's 1971 attempt. . . . [C]ompared to Hall's, the 1971 book seems arch, amateurish, and sketchy. . . . Where Pope Hennessy often obtrudes his epigrammatic cleverness, Hall is ever the deferential efficient servant of Trollope, who would doubtless have warmed to his latest chronicler's modesty, industry, and common sense.'[3]

Roger Kimball, in *The New Criterion*, writes, 'Throughout his book, Professor Hall is utterly responsible, competent, and not infrequently a bit dull.'[4]

John Halperin, in *Biography*, writes, 'Generally, Hall's is an excellent account of Trollope, as much of a page-turner as any of the 47 novels, as good as some of them, and totally absorbing.'[5]

Kimball faults what he considers plot summaries: '[Hall's] basic procedure, once Trollope has gotten around to publishing books, is to insert a potted summary of the latest volume every dozen pages or so. This is a perfectly normal operation of course, but *en masse* and without much effort to "place" Trollope in a larger literary context, it soon becomes tedious.'[6]

R.D. McMaster, in *Victorian Review*, says, 'Eschewing plot synopses "except in instances where they contribute to the narrative," Hall is adept at moving back and forth between Trollope's works and his life, as well as at placing the works in critical perspective.'[7]

Kimball is also troubled by the length of the book: 'Then, too, Professor Hall has allowed himself a great deal of repetition: readers encounter the same points, even some favorite quotations, again and again. Perhaps he would have done well to trim his manuscript by eighty or one hundred pages.'[8]

R.C. Terry in *Victorian Studies*, says, 'A fine job of compression has been achieved on a subject of huge proportions, and the telling is notable for its clarity and breadth of illustration.'[9]

By far the largest area of disagreement among reviewers concerned the problem of just how much analysis, speculation, or interpretation this or other biographies ought to attempt. In a one-page introduction to the book I began by quoting Trollope, 'The man of letters is, in truth, ever writing his own biography,' saying that I would accordingly frequently quote him, not only his letters and autobiography, but his novels, travel books, and essays. I said mine was not a 'thesis' biography, though I did have 'leading ideas about Trollope, which, while not straining to solve all the mysteries of the man, inform this work: . . . that Trollope was more of an intellect than is usually recognized; that his genius . . . was essentially a comic one; that he was a writer of care and judgment . . . that . . . he was one of the giants of English fiction.'[10] Everybody seemed to like the idea of not having a thesis. However, the phrase about 'not straining to solve all the mysteries of the man' occasioned considerable debate. My words were a quiet way of declaring that I eschew highly imaginative interpretation or speculation and certainly do not indulge in (terrible word) 'psychobiography'. Instead, I was announcing myself as a rather unobtrusive biographer. Of course I knew from the beginning that it was impossible to do anything other than write my own version of Trollope, that there is no single Trollope, that 'objectivity' is a word no longer used in regard to biography. We know that each biographer, out of the huge mass of material before him – letters, works, testimony of contemporaries, etc. – chooses that which shores up the image and ideas he or she already has of his subject and works. Still, some biographers are undeniably more analytic (if not psychoanalytic), more speculative, much more 'intrusive' than others. I am not saying – though I have my prejudice – that mine is the better choice; rather that, for good or ill, I was among the more cautious. Reviewers, as seems natural enough, are very much divided on this matter. I shall first clump together those who felt the book suffered from my hands-off approach:

Richard Eder, in the *Los Angeles Times* (5 December 1991), says that he would have preferred more speculation:

> Trollope scrupulously avoided any detailed self-revelation, except when writing of his miserable childhood. Accordingly there is next to nothing about his wife, Rose, and not much about his relationship with his two sons . . . [or with] Kate Field. . . . Hall extracts a suggestive portrait nevertheless, though I wish he had let himself go a little more in speculating about those areas, such as Trollope's marriage, that he could not document.

> Roger Kimball says, 'Professor Hall remarks in his introduction that he has not attempted to write a "thesis" biography. That is certainly

all to the good. But those familiar with the lineaments of Trollope's life are nonetheless likely to find Professor Hall's book most engaging when he steps back from his chronicle and offers an opinion.'[11] William St. Clair, in *The Financial Times* (9 November 1991), writes:

> Hall's approach is comprehensive. He sets out the established facts in chronological order with the minimum of unadventurous comment. The knowledge and industry he brings to his task are impressive, and the book is full of interest, particularly about Trollope's earlier years [R.C. Terry says 'In many ways the later chapters of Hall's biography are the most illuminating.'[12]] However, in declining to be drawn into speculation, selectivity, or interpretation, Hall has allowed the agenda of his book to be determined by the random pattern of survival of documents. . . . Occasionally Hall pulls together Trollope's comments on a topic, such as women, but the book as a whole too often betrays its origins in the card index and the PC. The book is an invaluable volume for reference but it is more a draft waiting to be shaped than a finished work of biographical literature. If we are to understand such a remarkable man as Trollope, we need more.

John Powell writes, 'N. John Hall accepts the bulk of Trollope's autobiographical writing at face value, rigorously following his footsteps, and refrains from attempting a comprehensive explanation of the "mysteries of the man." Indeed, one will hardly know that mysteries exist. However, having accepted Hall's clearly stated fundamentals, one may quickly forget to remember that there should be more.'[13]

Hugh David, in *The Times Saturday Review*, calls the book an 'efficient, if rather impersonal, biography,' saying that its author, 'the "Distinguished Professor of English, Bronx Community College," is . . . more interested in the works than in the personality behind them':

> Even though he had access to Trollope's uniquely detailed travel and work diaries, Hall seldom brings his subject to life. . . . [Anthony Burgess, in the *Independent* (11 October 1991), writes, 'It would seem impossible to make a compelling biography out of a life without major crises. Professor Hall . . . has performed this task admirably.' Commendably, however, Hall has 'no particular slant or angle on Trollope'. This is not, as he writes in his introduction, 'a "thesis" biography'.] It is a straightforward account of a fascinating

life – and the fact the Trollope emerges as something of grey man might just be one more reason for his continuing popularity at Number Ten [a reference to John Major's devotion to Trollope's fiction].[14]

Robert Bernard Martin, in *The New York Review of Books* (28 May 1992), declares that the new biographies (especially Hall's) have come up with merely external details, which, though useful for knowledge of limited aspects of Trollope's life, offer

> little hint of what kind of beliefs or compulsions or eccentricities prompted the works in the first place. They don't change our view of Trollope in any important way. The day-to-day slog of a writer's existence is often central to his life and hence an important part of literary biography, but it is not the most interesting part to the reader and must be smuggled in as ballast to any consideration of his creative imagination. Add to this information two or three pages of plot recapitulation on each of the forty-seven novels, and the total of detailed facts Professor Hall gives us lies heavily on the reader.

Martin lauds Hall's earlier edition of Trollope's letters, remarking that the depth of detailed information there brought to bear on the correspondence, along with Hall's 'insistence on ascertainable fact', fits very nicely with the 'buttoned-up, no-nonsense contents of the letters.' But he questions whether this approach is equally appropriate in a biography:

> It is not Hall's fault that his sources are so unrewarding, but biography dependent upon external event quickly runs dry unless it is accompanied by an attempt to understand motivation. He is quite right to distrust reckless guesswork, but informed speculation is part of what we expect from an expert: careful postulation made credible by what responsible evidence there is, of which the expert knows more than we. Too often in this book the reader worries fretfully about what the purpose of Hall's research is if it doesn't suggest new ways of thinking about either Trollope or his fiction. . . .
> But if Trollope left little indication of a fertile inner life, we can hardly help feeling that its potential has been refined and channeled into the rich legacy of novels he left. Professor Hall will have nothing to do with psychological guesswork about his subject. Since his major source of basic information is Trollope's

Autobiography, and that is so notably reticent, he is often forced into elaborating what has already been told more concisely.

Martin offers examples: Trollope names sixteen members whom he met at the Cosmopolitan Club, and 'Hall expands the list to twenty-four.' While on a trip abroad Trollope visited twenty-five places, each recorded here, with Hall setting down 'on the same page' a list of eighteen foreign settings Trollope used in his fiction: 'It all feels accurate enough and comes of close reading of the novels, but is perilously close to cruelty to the reader.'

On the other hand: Douglas Fetherling, in the *Kingston Whig Standard* (31 October 1992), says, 'Prof. Hall doesn't plunge into speculation. He simply rereads all the works, gathers every scrap of factual information, and organizes the results into a narrative that rattles along pleasantly and instructively in a manner one is tempted to call Trollopean.'

John Bayley, in the *Times Literary Supplement* (8 November 1991), writes:

Professor Hall's narrative is remarkably well suited to his subject's style and personality, 'never forcing itself on the attention of the reader' (a contemporary critic's praise for Trollope's own writing) and full of the sort of well chosen detail that not only complements Trollopian 'literariness' but fleshes out the in some ways oddly abstract nature of his daily invention. . . . Without being invidious, one may say that Hall's biography is more satisfying than [certain others] in its method and scholarship but still more in its quiet good nature and low authorial profile. Trollope would have liked it.

R. D. McMaster writes:

The biography is full of detail, including frequent quotation from Victorian reviews of Trollope's work, without ever seeming pedantic. Hall's presentation of Trollope's dynamic personality is thoroughly engrossing. . . . And if the biography has a special focus of interest, as opposed to a 'thesis', it may be seen in Hall's even-handed exploration of [the] opposing tendencies in Trollope the man and Trollope the artist. Hall is concerned to let Trollope reveal himself 'not only from his letters and posthumously published autobiography but also from his fiction.' With forty-seven novels there is plenty of room.[15]

James R. Kincaid in the *New York Times Book Review* (22 December 1991) says:

Writing with a quiet precision much like Trollope's, Mr. Hall does not so much argue a thesis as allow us access to a life and art both compelling and deeply moving. . . .

Trollope's [loud, aggressive personal style] is, doubtless, compensatory, a shield for his 'inner vulnerable self,' but Mr. Hall is not interested in imprisoning his subject in psychological traps. Instead he lets roar at us a Trollope who took control even of his own defensive maneuvers, made them work, turned them into considerable delight and profit. It's as if this boomingly unneurotic Trollope were telling the story, and not Mr. Hall. Mr. Hall doesn't even warn us to hold on to our hats, and his rich and extensive historical scholarship is employed with such self-effacing grace that we almost think it came unbidden. . . .

No writer has written more piercingly about his childhood than Trollope, and Mr. Hall opens it all up for us by some very unobtrusive pointing. . . . Mr. Hall allows all this poignant material to speak largely for itself, mentioning simply that 'if a child feels lonely, persecuted, bullied, neglected, and at times abandoned by his parents, it does no good to say that, looked at from another perspective, things were really not so bad.' Mr. Hall is a master at keeping from adopting these 'other perspectives' that would muffle the great power available in what we are convinced is Trollope's own view of the matter.

Finally, Walter Kendrick in the *Voice Literary Supplement* also takes up the theme of intrusiveness:

N. John Hall's *Trollope: A Biography* . . . adheres to no theory and admits to no method; Hall's aim is merely to chronicle what Trollope did and to determine with all possible exactness when and where he did it. With restraint that's either admirable or stick-in-the-mud, depending on your point of view, he resists the temptation of Trollope's spectacularly miserable childhood, which any psychobiographer (for that matter, any biographer less modest than Hall) would leap upon, scalpel ready. . . .

Hall details [Trollope's monumental energy] with irreproachable thoroughness; he even manages to make it entertaining. Reversing the psychobiographer's method, he reads Trollope's life out of his fiction, looking there for evidence of Trollope's feelings about parents, children, sex, and love, all the intimate matters that the real-life record leaves blank. The result is a triumphantly superficial *Trollope*, which needs nothing but the rich bright surface to justify itself and to satisfy the reader's curiosity. Hall's method is Boswellian in that sense, and something of a throwback; it might not work for anyone but 'so honourable and interesting a man,' as a friend of Trollope's judged him to be. Yet Hall's unassuming stance also precludes any claim that *Trollope* explains Trollope, accounts for his work, or places either in some overarching theoretical scheme. *Trollope* rings true, but then Trollope always insisted his novels were, too. *Trollope* could be called *Novel #48.* . . .

Hall exemplifies the paradoxical figure of today's biographer-as-artist. With no evident bias or agenda, he compels admiration for himself as well as his subject, simply through writerly skill. This is Hall's inevitable self-portrait: knowing that no biographer can avoid painting one, he makes himself out to be a cheerful, trustworthy impresario, who draws back the curtain of a drama of guaranteed interest.[16]

I have given equal space to the negative and the positive. And although it was perhaps ungenerous of me to allow the favorable reviews to go last, I have dutifully refrained from pointing out the fatuousness and self-contradictions of some of the negative comments. The whole business reminds me of Thomas Hardy's delightful 1907 letter to Clement Shorter:

> I endeavour to profit from the opinions of those wonderful youths and maidens, my reviewers, & am laying to heart a few infallible truths taught by them: e.g., –
>
> That T.H's verse is his only claim to notice.
> That T.H's prose is his only real work.
> That T.H's early novels are best.
> That T.H's later novels are best.
> That T.H's novels are good in plot & bad in character.
> That T.H's novels are bad in plot & good in character.
> That T.H's philosophy is all that matters.
> That T.H.'s writings are good in spite of their bad philosophy.
>
> This is as far as I have got at present, but I struggle gallantly on.[17]

But I shall now cheat by adding a little coda, one last favorable excerpt. Fairness has its limits. Here are the closing two sentences from Anthony Burgess's review for the *Independent* (11 October 1991). As far as I know, the latter sentiment, at least, remains uncontradicted by any other reviewer: 'This fine biography is a kind of thanksgiving. And the world it describes must be very comforting to a man who works in the Bronx.'

4

The Necrophiliac Art?

MARTIN STANNARD

Modern biography might be said to have begun with Lytton Strachey's *Eminent Victorians* (1918). From that point, irreverence became fashionable. A decade later, amid the huge backwash of chatty subjectivity that often replaced the Victorian memoir, Roy Campbell could remark that: 'The tradition of modern biography is to search for incompatibilities: to adopt a tone of indulgent irony towards one's subject: and to rely on a slick, slightly epigrammatical, journalistic style to carry it off. At its supreme moments it provokes one to a mischievous titter. . . . It is the most perfect instrument that has yet been invented to enable the mediocre to patronise the great.'[1] He was reviewing Evelyn Waugh's first book, a life of Rossetti. Neither Campbell nor Waugh could be accused of undue reverence towards his elders. It is interesting to note, then, that Campbell absolves *Rossetti* from his general condemnation. Why? Perhaps because, if Waugh had not solved the problems of modern biography, he had at least addressed them. And the difficulties Waugh itemized in writing this kind of book – of tone, of ironical distance from one's subject, of one's location within or between conventional generic boundaries – are still with us.

In Waugh's view there were two alternative approaches, neither of them satisfactory. There was the Victorian model: the two-volume eulogy, designed 'to assist with our fathers' decorum at the lying-in-state of our great men': no sex, no scandal, no self-doubt on the part of either subject or writer, an heroic portrait of moral rectitude 'cleansed of all the stains of humanity.'[2] Then there was the post-Strachey style: anti-heroic, psychoanalytic; sex, scandal and the *subject's* self-doubt to the fore, the whole presented with an air of easy self-confidence by the writer. 'The corpse,' Waugh suggested, 'has become the marionette. With bells on its fingers and wires on its toes it is jigged about to a "period dance" of our own piping.'[3] The modern style, then, was manipulative of historical 'fact,' often divorcing itself from the subject's views of his or her own life. This has remained the prevalent fashion. '[O]nly by understanding the life apart from the subject's self-proclaimed image,' Joyce Carol Oates states, 'can one write a meaningful biography, as triumphant in its creative achievement as any work of fiction.'4 Here's the rub. Is biography fact or fiction, historical document or dramatized 'documentary'?

One approach to this problem is provided by Michael Holroyd. In a 1992 interview he suggested that biography is a genre. The relationship between biographer and subject, he says, is like a marriage 'in that you commit yourself at the beginning but you don't really know how it will turn out.'5 Some literary lives, such as Gittings's account of Hardy, can prove distressing for readers. 'Would they be able to read the work with as much pleasure as before? I think such questions are sentimental. They make a very unsophisticated connection between life and work.'6 The attitude here is distinctly 'modern' and seems perfectly reasonable. Biographers are not in the business of protecting the cherished image of a cultural hero. They are concerned with the truth. If that is offensive, then so be it. Michael Sheldon would surely agree. The image of the marriage, however, carries with it additional implications. If the biographer is wedded to his subject, this suggests not merely his commitment to serious research but also the reciprocation of the subject. An intimacy between subject and writer is implied which can be construed positively or negatively. A positive construction might argue that this empathy is a precondition of all good literary biography; a negative, that such reciprocation is wholly imaginary, self-seeking, a kind of aesthetic masturbation.

It is often remarked that in our 'postmodern' age, the collapse of the realist novel has left a gap in the market. Readers who prefer a plain tale, authoritatively told, turn to biography for the security of well-drawn characters, a hero or heroine, and satisfying closure. Just as the eighteenth- and nineteenth-century novel often masqueraded as biography ('The Life and Adventures of . . . '), so biographies today can masquerade as novels. Novelists (Peter Ackroyd, A.N. Wilson, Alan Judd) turn increasingly to biography, experimenting with the form. Ackroyd's invented conversations with Dickens, or Judd's imagined meeting with Ford in heaven, break from the convention of the biographer as objective historian to emphasize his role as enthusiast, fellow-traveller, and, above all, as artist. The narrator in these books often takes on the function of the omniscient, intrusive narrator of realist fiction.

The relationship between biographer and subject is thus crucial to our understanding of the form. Holroyd points to its two 'father-figures': Boswell with his life of Johnson, and Johnson himself with his *Lives of the English Poets*. Holroyd believes that he belongs to the Johnsonian tradition. The energy of Boswell's narrative depends upon his 'presence' ('His work comes wonderfully alive whenever he himself is on the page'). Johnson's, by implication, relies more on the analysis of a 'sort of political, cultural and artistic history of the times' as context for his subject. 'Inevitably, like a portrait painter, you put a little of yourself into the portrait . . . but you must retain a historical perspective and independence of judgement.'[7]

One might take this further and detect a fashionable trend in the subjective, 'Boswellian' style of biography which is either written by an acquaintance of the subject or by someone who craves acquaintance through the act of writing. This kind of book often sets its face against the 'scholarly,' or 'Johnsonian', Life. Reading Alan Judd's *Ford Madox Ford* immediately after Arthur P. Mizener's *The Saddest Story*, for instance, one is struck by the recurrent antagonism between academe and 'professional writers.' Judd is irritated by what he takes to be Mizener's cumbersome pedantry. Mizener, we are told, is always 'negative,' always carping, correcting, offering ungenerous constructions of Ford's behavior. For Mizener, his subject is a complex of contradictions. Ford is a great writer in patches, a bad one when churning out books to stay alive, a self-deluder, generous, 'romantic,' but rather vain and pompous. Judd, in contrast, is in love with his subject: Ford can do no wrong. He is a comrade foolishly abused by literary enemies, ex-lovers, and packs of scavenging dons.

The same rift emerged more recently. Since Gittings, there have been two major biographies of Hardy: one (by Michael Millgate) rigorously academic, the other (by Martin Seymour-Smith) passionate and subjective. The latter, taken to task in the *Times Literary Supplement*, found a defender:

> Sir – Samuel Hynes devotes the first third of his review . . . to his own thought on various 'cruxes' in Hardy's work, and to frank speculations. . . . He then attacks Seymour-Smith for intruding his own opinions into the biography. But this is the whole point: Seymour-Smith is a poet and working writer, and his book has a frankly 'inside' perspective, rather than an academic 'outside' one: he identifies with Hardy. . . . [He] does not appropriate his subject in the academic way, making it an object of licensed

possession. . . . Hynes complains: 'In Seymour-Smith's populist view, professors are the enemies of the literary values he is defending. But in reality, most of them aren't; they are rather his allies.' But on the evidence of Hynes's review, academics and working writers are not allies; they are at war. What Hynes condescendingly . . . calls Seymour-Smith's 'populism' is evident in *Hardy* as a respect for the non-academic readers who are the true allies of writers and have decided that Hardy's books survive. When the economic crunch comes, they may also decide whether universities should be paid out of taxes to finance literary criticism and editing – a stage of the war I personally look forward to.[8]

Strong, if not entirely rational, stuff. (Does a working writer's identification with his subject automatically guarantee him immunity from prosecution? Aren't academics 'working writers,' especially if, like Sheldon, they are paid large advances by their publishers?) Nevertheless, the terms are interesting. Each side in this debate accuses the other of subjectivism and, implicitly or directly, of unfairly appropriating the subject as 'an object of licensed possession.' Broadly speaking, Holroyd's gentlemanly distinction describes the opposing factions in a war between those who adopt high ground as artists or as intellectuals. In our tabloid age, when neither the artist nor the intellectual has much impact, both have often relinquished idealism and descended into the field of battle for an unholy scrap. Sheldon's attempt to demolish Graham Greene's moral probity presents us not with a marriage between biographer and subject but with a murderer and victim. The effect of the book is to present Greene as a hypocrite.

Feelings run high in this conflict. And it is not simply between 'professional writers' and academics. It also divides living subjects from unauthorized biographers, executors from authorized biographers, and the reading public from biographers critical of their subjects. Both Doris Lessing and Muriel Spark have felt obliged to produce autobiographies in an attempt to stem a flood of misinformation. One thinks of the troubled negotiations between Bernard Crick and Sonia Orwell, between Anne Stevenson and Ted and Olwyn Hughes.[9] Indeed, there are many who are angered by the whole notion of literary biography. To them this 'genre' becomes a contemptible form of voyeurism. Germaine Greer has found herself in much the same position as Lessing. Having had the temerity to become a famous writer, she now discovers that her life, in addition to her writings, is somehow assumed to be public property: 'On the writer's carcase, and in the writer's guts, live many parasitic organisms. Some, publishers and agents for example, are genuinely symbiotic useful creatures. Others – broadcasters, interviewers and the like – who get much more than they give, are fake symbiotic. Then there are the biographers of living writers, who are the intellectual equivalent of flesh-eating bacterium. . . . Dead writers cannot defend themselves. . . . The literary biographer who munches on a living writer . . . announces to the world that she cannot get what she wants – riches, fame and power – by her own efforts and has to hitch her wagon to someone who works harder or to better effect.'[10]

There are moral questions at stake here, questions of property and propriety. It is not simply a matter of defending lily-livered writers or executors from the ugliness of truth. It concerns, essentially, the invasion of privacy by the telephoto lens of the uninvited guest. 'The transgressive nature of biography', as Janet Malcolm points out, 'is rarely acknowledged, but it is the only explanation for biography's status as a popular genre. The reader's amazing tolerance (which he would extend to no novel written half as badly as most biographies) makes sense only when seen as a kind of collusion between him and the biographer in an excitingly forbidden undertaking: tiptoeing down the corridor together, to stand in front of the bedroom door and try to peep through the keyhole.'[11] These are, perhaps, unpleasant realities which biographers should face about themselves. How many of us could pretend that we do not enjoy reading other people's letters? 'Biography,' Malcolm insists, 'is the medium through which the remaining secrets of the famous dead are taken from them and dumped out in full view of the world.'[12] Viewed like this, the notion of the 'marriage' between biographer and subject is wilfully self-deceiving, the defense of the rapist or necrophile.

It is easy to sympathize with the living writer persecuted by some parasite rooting about in her private life. For Greer, her friends' response to her tormentor's enquiries has become a test of their loyalty. 'I will interpret collaboration,' she says, 'as meaning that our friendship is of no further value to them.'[13] What lies behind this is fundamental: common human decency. 'All living human beings have the right to invent themselves. It is not the prerogative of writers to re-invent living people in their own terms.'[14] She feels this particularly strongly because when her husband sold his version of her life, she made the mistake of reading it and nearly went mad. The image there bore no relation to her self-image. Oates might well reply to this,

'Well, it wouldn't, would it? Nor should it.' But Greer surely has a point. The tabloid attitude to the famous embarrassed by 'revelations' is usually the cynical: 'If you don't like the heat. . . . ' If you court publicity, you are public property. This is surely an intolerable moral position and leads to the absurdities of 'virtual biography' like Joe McGinniss's 'life' of Senator Kennedy, *The Last Brother.* It is presumably only a matter of time before this technique is extended with the full panoply of postmodern defense to literary lives. Ackroyd might be said to have begun it already. New Journalism has much to answer for in this respect. Its feebler adherents have brought the art of biography into disrepute. If we abandon the precept of thorough documentation, there is nothing we cannot write about the dead, and careful phrasing can extend a similar liberty to defamation of the living. One further trick in this book has become a legal *cause célèbre*: David Leavitt's re-writing of Spender's life in his novel *While England Sleeps.*

At the root of all this lies that most awkward of questions: 'Who owns a life?' The dangerous attraction of Greer's argument is that it extends beyond the condemnation of the persecution of the living. *All* biographers, it seems, are in her view pie-dogs, the lowest form of literary life. In this, she is articulating an ancient grudge with solid provenance. George Eliot described biography as a 'disease of English literature.'[15] Something, she insisted, 'should be done by dispassionate criticism towards the reform of . . . literary biography. Is it not odious that as soon as a man is dead his desk is raked, and every insignificant memorandum which he never meant for the public, is printed for the gossiping amusement of people too idle to re-read his books? . . . It is something like the uncovering of the dead Byron's club foot.'[16] Ted Hughes apparently feels much the same: 'It is infuriating for me to see my private experiences and feelings re-invented for me, in that crude, bland unanswerable way, and interpreted and published as official history. . . . And to see her [Plath] used in the same way.'[17] If we can't get it right about the living, what chance do we have with the even more remote dead? Were they to rear up from their graves, would they not turn a weary eye on us and say, 'That is not what I meant at all. That is not it, at all'?

There is, of course, an equally weary postmodern response: no one owns a life, can, or should attempt to, 'possess' it. No one knows another. Facts are relative to the point of view from which they are constructed. The sign is arbitrary. But Anne Stevenson surely humanizes this, rescues the position from the recklessness of virtual biography, when she says: 'I do not agree with Alvarez, with Plath and with Ted Hughes (perhaps) when they contend that the pursuit of the absolute has anything to do with the pursuit of truth. Truth is, in its nature, multiple and contradictory, part of the flux of history, untrappable in language. The only real road to truth is through doubt and tolerance.'[18] Given that it is the 'crude, bland, unanswerable' tone of biographical narrative which most irritates its victims, perhaps we might find a partial answer to the problem in demolishing the pretense of being the omniscient narrator of a realist fiction. Add to that the guarantee that there will be no speculation without documentation and we might be getting somewhere.

These issues came to mind when I read the (thankfully few) negative reviews of my biography of Waugh. I suppose one should not be surprised that different readers read differently, but I found myself wondering whether my antagonists had read the book, or whether the book was so badly written as to convey an impression of my subject which was quite the opposite of that intended. All believed that I hated Waugh. Resentment streamed from the high ground of cultural patronage ('Stannard, who teaches Eng. Lit. Crit. in the Midlands . . .').[19] I was the poor chap who couldn't understand the inflections of upper-class humor, the backbiter, the underdog snapping at the heels of his betters. I was, of course, the academic, one of those who could not 'do' and therefore taught. One reviewer entitled his piece: 'Hooper's Revenge.'[20] Christopher Hawtree, in an otherwise generous assessment, compared Mark Gerson's photographs of Waugh and myself: 'Thirty years on, with Mark [sic] Stannard before his lens, one might wonder whether any thought crossed [Gerson's] mind about the reaction of Waugh's shade to his latest biographer, for the back flap reveals a shirt-sleeved man with a moustache, blow-dried hair, and a penchant for net-curtains which would never have sullied Piers Court or Combe Florey.'[21] I felt like writing back, pointing out that Waugh often sported a moustache, that I didn't blow-dry my hair and that the net curtains belonged to Gerson's rather elegant address off Regent's Park Road. But what was the point? Why drag me into it? Why drag an invented me into it?

I puzzled over this and my conclusions brought me back to Holroyd. He is right, surely, when he says that the biographer leaves something of himself in the portrait (Waugh tells us a great deal about himself in *Rossetti*). Perhaps I had left too much. Nevertheless, I began to wonder how well the biographer can control either the 'marriage' with his subject or the struggle for objectivity. As with all marriages, the relationship is never untroubled. It is an abiding, tempered love, rather than infatuation, which keeps the biographer going. I, too, would think of my work, however humbly, as belonging to the Johnsonian tradition of cultural debate. The only justification of literary biography for me is that it should enlighten the reader about the subject's art, provide a mental landscape to historicize critical interpretation. Ultimately it is, or should be, an act of literary criticism. I did not know Waugh. I don't inhabit his 'world.' I am not in sympathy with his hatred of the 'Common Man'. I am not a Catholic. But I have a huge admiration for his writing, roar with laughter at his jokes and eccentricities, admire his brutal honesty. In short, we often love, or at least respect, those who challenge our assumptions – so long as there is a saving grace. And Waugh certainly had the latter: a powerful humility beneath that façade of arrogance. It is probably true that he would not have liked me. Does this matter? Clearly it did to those reviewers who seem to have felt that Waugh would have liked them. I, however, don't believe the question to be relevant, and that to drag an imagined 'me' into reviews is 'to make a very unsophisticated connection between life and work,' not only between Waugh's life and work but also between my life and his, my life and his work, and, ultimately, between my life and my work.

Having said all this, there remains a problem. Does the reader of biography demand that the subject be eternally cast in the role of hero? The Boswellian biographers, writing a form of fiction in which their 'presence' is crucial, run fewer risks of embarrassing us with unpleasant contradictions. Rather, they comfort us with the assumption that their hero or heroine is both 'knowable' and likeable: that if we had met the subject, he or she would have liked both the biographer and us. The Johnsonian version is cooler. Here the biographer is equally in the position of persuasion, but rather more in the role of entertaining barrister than that of autobiographer or novelist. A certain distance is preserved, but if he acts (as I think he should) as counsel for the defense and the prosecution, the jury may well react against this performance with puzzlement and irritation. It is here that the legal analogy collapses. For where a jury has no acquaintance with the defendant, the reader of biography usually brings to the subject all the baggage of a previous relationship. I had not realized just how passionate this relationship can be. Reviewers of biographies, for instance, often have a 'theory' about the subject and spend most of their time explaining it. Even to suggest the logical inconsistency of some of your subject's arguments can be tantamount to insulting a reader's most cherished beliefs.

There is, it seems, no escaping the fact that readers of biography often turn to it, not in the spirit of free enquiry, but to support preconceptions, and that the contradiction of these notions represents an insult to both subject and reader. No matter how even-handed you try to be with the evidence, there are always two stories being told: that of your subject, and that of your relationship with your subject. The biographer can never eradicate that tone of voice which reveals him as a participant in the narrative, nor should he. But while I support Holroyd's ideal of 'passionate detachment,' I wonder whether it is achievable. And while I applaud Stevenson's notion of 'truth' as 'multiple and contradictory,' I wonder whether the construction of a readable narrative imbued with that 'voice' can avoid a tone of 'authority'. Can we assume the authority of objective commentators while simultaneously undermining it by admitting to the arbitrary nature of 'truth'? Leon Edel once remarked that 'A biographer is a storyteller who may not invent his facts but who is allowed to imagine his form.'[22] Perhaps that is the closest we can come to a resolution of this dilemma. Biography is, I believe, an art, and an art precisely because it gains its effects by the imagination of its form. But if we are going to discuss it as a genre, perhaps it would be as well to acknowledge that many readers are determined to see it as a form of autobiography. And that they might be right.

5

Read that Countenance

CATHERINE AIRD

Literary biography is by definition the outcome of the study of the life and work of an author and, *ipso facto*, the study of the interaction between that life and that work. One of the problems most commonly met with in constructing the literary biography is that, in the main, the life of an author is a sedentary and outwardly uneventful one and of necessity often an isolated existence as well.

One way of approaching this, of course, is to let the Biblical view prevail and be deemed sufficient for the biographer's purpose: 'By their fruits shall ye know them' which was certainly so in the case of the Good Samaritan.

And sometimes – although not always – there is such written richness that the biographer can take to heart Rudyard Kipling's command in his poem 'The Appeal':

> And for the little, little span
> The dead are borne in mind,
> Seek not to question other than
> The books I leave behind.

There is another view, though, which is that anything at all which assists in the exploration of 'the mind of the maker' is worthy of consideration. And what, since the fifteenth century at least, is left behind by most literary subjects in addition to their writings is the representation of a face.

Faces were, of course, delineated well before the fifteenth century but not often in a manner from which accurate deductions can be made. There was, for example, a convention in the Greek Archaic period in the sixth century B.C. for human statues to be represented smiling. This drawing of the mouth upwards in a curve became known as 'the archaic smile,' which was described as an expression of 'strained

41

cheerfulness.' It cannot have mirrored the true likeness (or feeling) in every single case, and says more about the sculptors and their states of mind.[1]

Indeed the intervention between artist and subject is a known complication. The skills and weaknesses of amateur or professional sculptor, limner and photographer can and do come between biographer and subject, sometimes when it is far too late to 'say them nay.' The camera can lie.

It could be, too, that the artist sees what the biographer does not – the controversial portrait of Sir Winston Churchill in old age by Graham Sutherland, destroyed by Lady Churchill, is an instance of this. Equally those who view a painting may be divided on what they see in it. Leonardo da Vinci's Mona Lisa, described by Walter Pater as 'older than the rocks among which she sits,' has always been the subject of great debate.

Nevertheless in portraiture there are ever considerations of style, fashion, grooming, pose, setting, and other figures in the composition to be taken into account before a balanced judgement about the subject can be made. Hamlet's comment to Ophelia on women's make-up is not irrelevant: 'I have heard of your paintings, too, well enough. God has given you one face and you make yourselves another' (III.i.150).

In fact, all the foregoing can be affected by how the sitter wishes to be seen. Not every patron wishes to emulate Oliver Cromwell's injunction:

> Mr Lely, I desire you would use all your skill to paint my picture truly like me, and not flatter me at all; but remark all these roughnesses, pimples, warts, and everything as you see me, otherwise I will never pay a farthing for it.[2]

On the other hand King Edward VIII thought his left profile the better and insisted on the breaking of the convention of the monarch's head on coins facing the opposite way to that of his predecessor.

It is perhaps mostly in portraiture that the inherent dangers of stereotyping arise but even the least perceptive viewer of the famous last painting of Queen Elizabeth I, the Corsham Court portrait, cannot fail to infer her condition at the time. Attributed to Marcus Gheeraerts, it depicts the ageing, ill Queen, heavy head on hand, and is crowded with pessimistic symbolism – Father Time with his scythe is visible over one shoulder while the grinning figure of Death leers over the other.

More subtle is the fact that shop window displays of clocks always show the time at ten minutes to two because that presents a friendly face. Salespeople, psychologists all, know that were the hands to be set at twenty minutes past eight, the clock would not be bought.

There is little debate, though, about the interpretation of the body's construction on the face. In health there is ruddiness and well-being, approximate age can be determined, as usually can ethnicity and stature, and sometimes what Thomas Hardy described so marvellously in his poem 'Heredity':

> I am the family face;
> Flesh perishes, I live on,
> Projecting trait and trace
> Through time to times anon,
> And leaping from place to place
> Over oblivion.

In ill-health the picture is clearer still. Many physical diseases are visible in the face, including myxoedema and Graves disease, myasthenia gravis, Parkinson's Disease, the ravages of cancer, agromegaly, the after-effects of a stroke and Cushing's Syndrome (and, indeed, steroid therapy which produces a similar appearance). The effects of other medical treatment are sometimes apparent, too, and leave their mark on the facial appearance. And so does pain.

The argument thus far is scarcely contentious. A much more interesting dimension is postulated by William Shakespeare in *Macbeth* when Duncan says to Macbeth:

> There's no art
> To find the mind's construction
> in the face.
>
> [I.i.12–13]

(It would have been better from the biographer's point of view had the words been put in the mouth of the doctor in attendance upon Lady Macbeth, since Shakespeare's doctors are agreed by most commentators to have been particularly well-drawn.)[3]

There may, as Duncan says, be no art in the matter, but there is, of course, some science in doing so – and perhaps some pseudo-science too. First identified in 1569 there was the practice, which must have been known to Shakespeare, of metoposcopy, defined as 'the art of judging character or of telling a fortune by the forehead or face.'

Phrenology, 'the scientific study or theory of the mental faculties' came much later, in 1815, and hypothesizes that the mental powers of the individual consist of separate faculties, each having its organ and location in a definite region of the surface of the brain. (Modern research has demonstrated that this is so within the brain but is not outwardly visible.)

The anatomists named what they identified as 'the muscles of expression' with appropriate descriptions. The principal muscle groups in showing surprise and wonder have been named the *corrugator supercilii*, whilst those demonstrating the curling of the lip in hatred and contempt are the *orbicularis (triangularis) oris*. Puzzlement is seen as a contraction of the *occipito frontalis*.

It is these and other muscles that reflect the emotions of composure, veneration, fear and terror, scorn and derision. These feelings are physical manifestations of perfectly normal and quite rational reactions experienced by the subject – and most of the human race – from time to time in response to particular stimuli and stresses; and which were studied so extensively by Charles Darwin in his *The Expression of Emotion in Man and Animals* (1872). In the second half of the present century much not dissimilar work has been done on what is now known as 'body language.'

There are also the facial responses of the mind in disease. As Robert Burton observed in his *Anatomy of Melancholy* (1621) the visage reflects abnormal and aberrant emotions too. He painted a classic picture of the face in depression when he wrote:

Although they may be uncommonly lean, hirsute, uncheerful in countenance, withered and not so pleasant to behold, by reason of those continual fears, griefs and vexations, dull, heavy, lazy, restless, unapt to go about any business: yet their memories are for the most part good. . . .

That madness left its mark on the face is evidenced by the series of studies of heads of lunatics painted by the French artist Gericault in the late eighteenth century.

Cesaro Lombroso (1836–1909), one of the founders of the science of criminology, went much, much further and postulated that the physical construction of the faces of criminals showed similar common characteristics, and thus reflected the cast of mind of the subject. The men and women about whom he wrote were members of what he identified as 'the criminal classes' but even he did not attempt to distinguish whether the criminality was the cause of the shape of the face or the shape of the face the cause of the criminality.

Another Victorian criminologist of a similar persuasion was the American, Henry M. Boies, who wrote in 1893:

Everyone who has visited prisons and observed large numbers of prisoners together has undoubtedly been impressed, from the appearance of the prisoners alone, that a large proportion of them were born to be criminals.[4]

Whilst the modern observer does not necessarily associate – as Lombroso did – a prognathous projecting lower jaw with aggression, more will think twice before concluding that a receding chin is not always the sign of weakness. The latter belief (if not misconception) is underlined by the frequency with which the operation correcting this is performed by plastic surgeons and the persistent use of the epithet 'chinless' as derogatory.

Similarly, 'high-brow' is a term meant to indicate both intelligence and intellectual refinement and 'low-brow' its converse. This is the result of an observation, now enshrined as fact in many minds, that the greater the distance of the top of the head from above the ears the more brain there is between those same ears. A high-domed forehead is also felt to indicate great brain-power.

Reading Shakespeare's mind is, of course, no easy matter. In fact the statement 'there's no art' is capable of two mutually incompatible constructions: 'there's no art' being perceived to mean either that it is too easy to require skill or that it is too difficult and therefore impossible to do.

The context inclines towards the former interpretation. It deals with the execution of Cawdor. When Duncan has asked Malcolm if it has been done, Malcolm reports how well Cawdor has died after confessing and repenting his treasons and says:

Nothing in his life
Became him like the leaving it; he died
As one that had been studied in his death,
To throw away the dearest thing he owed,
As 'twere a careless trifle.

Duncan responds:

> There's no art
> To find the mind's construction in the face:
> He was a gentleman on whom I built
> An absolute trust.
>
> [I.iv.7–15]

It is not too difficult to enumerate the contributory factors which influence the reading of a face. To establish whether or not it is possible to know the heart or mind of the human being behind it from that face alone is quite another matter.

There is what almost amounts to an interdiction against doing either in the Old Testament when the Lord says to Samuel:

> Look not on his countenance, or on the height of his stature; because I have refused him: for the Lord seeth not as man seeth; for man looketh on the outward appearance, but the LORD looketh on the heart.   (I Samuel 16:7)

What is incontrovertible is that no human being can look upon the countenance of another without forming some conclusion about its owner, albeit subconsciously – usually within seconds and employing instinct rather than reason. This can have far-reaching implications. Sir Edward Grey, Foreign Secretary of Great Britain in the First World War, used the fact in an argument against the development of picture papers when he wrote in an address called 'The Pleasures of Reading':

> I found the other day a person who during the war between the Turks and the Greeks expressed an opinion rather in favour of the Turks, because he or she (I will not reveal even the sex) said that, judging by the pictures, Mustapha Kemal looked rather a good sort of fellow.[5]

This is an experience not lost on those who mastermind political propaganda. It should not be ignored by biographers and other writers.

Charlotte Brontë also postulated the connection between physical appearance and the person when she caused Madame Beck, one of the characters in *Villette*, to say: 'I want your opinion. We know your skill in physiognomy; use it now. Read that countenance.'[6]

It is not easy.

6

Reflections on Writing the Plath Biography

LINDA WAGNER-MARTIN

Having written or edited nearly thirty academic books which had been published by university presses, I assumed that writing commercial biography would be similar. I had spent parts of several years reading the unpublished Plath materials at Indiana University (Mrs Plath had sold her immense collection of letters to and from Sylvia, manuscripts, and memorabilia to the Lilly Library there in 1979). Few scholars had used this collection. When the even larger Plath archive opened in the Rare Book Room at Smith College, materials that had been collected and sold to Smith by Ted Hughes, it seemed the right time to propose a new biography. I would have access to much new material, and I felt the compelling need to present Sylvia Plath as a very bright, ambitious woman of the 1950s, whose desire to be a wife and mother as well as a writer was passionate but in no way 'abnormal.' The occurrences of depression that marked her life after her junior year in college, and again after the births of her children in 1960 and 1962, were isolated, and with proper treatment should not have led to her suicide in February of 1963 when she had just turned thirty. Above all, I wanted the book to reassure young women who were trying to become writers that it was not their writing that would depress them. Writing her great last poems, and taking what some critics had been calling 'psychic risks,' whatever that meant, had not killed Sylvia Plath. Her depression had killed her.

Perhaps I should have paid attention to several kinds of warnings. In publishing circles, people already spoke of the 'curse' of the Plath biography. At least three women scholars had already been given good advances by good publishers to write the Plath story. The first 'authorized' biographer worked for eight years under constraints from the estate that were impossible to meet. The last of the three books

47

sits still at its publisher's, the author having given up attempts to satisfy the estate. The second – and perhaps the most accomplished – author not only left her book unfinished, but left the literary field entirely. An early biography had appeared in 1976, and there were a dozen academic books about Plath's writing, as well as collections of essays on her work; so there was activity. Biography, however, continued to be a problem.

In writing Plath's biography, one comes under the amazingly tight control of the Plath estate, Ted Hughes and his older sister Olwyn Hughes, who was the literary executor of Sylvia Plath's writing for twenty-five years. (She has recently given up that position, but during the years of my preparing the book and negotiating with the estate, it was Olwyn who was completely in charge.) Olwyn, who lived in France during the three years that Ted and Sylvia lived in England before Plath's suicide, not only did not know her sister-in-law well; she also had no training in literature. The two women also were said to dislike each other. So the hands that controlled all Plath permissions were scarcely impartial, and once Hughes became Poet Laureate of England, the estate had political and literary power – at least in England – to back its decisions.

Because Plath died intestate, all rights and property went to Hughes, even though she was in the process of divorcing him. (He and Olwyn claim that he may have been reconciling with Sylvia, but British friends of Plath say she had moved beyond the separation stage and had already signed divorce papers, or was ready to sign them. Nothing remains, either in her papers or at her solicitor's – a lawyer who is now Hughes's lawyer – to indicate whether or not she was proceeding with the divorce.) Not only does any scholar apply to the Hugheses for all permissions to quote even from Plath's published poems and letters, but Hughes also has agreements with both the British and American publishers of Plath's work that their companies will give no permissions – of even the most routine kind – until (then) Olwyn had approved both the project and the person requesting permissions. This unusual situation has nothing to do with finances (the estate's charges for reprinting Plath's work are reasonable); it has to do entirely with control of what is being written. Even for brief essays about Plath's poetry, Olwyn asked to see the entire work rather than only the pages with quoted lines, the usual procedure, before she gave approval. And her custom was to take from one to three years to answer even the most ordinary requests for permission, a strategy that not only slowed publication but threatened it altogether.

No one except Ted (and Olwyn) Hughes can give permission for any use of either Plath's writing – published or unpublished – or any materials connected with her. All of her letters, of course, are theirs (in copyright law, the receiver of a letter owns the physical letter but not its contents), and letters written to Plath, because she has received them, are also the estate's. When Aurelia Plath, Sylvia's mother, tried to publish a collection of Sylvia's letters to her and her son (*Letters Home by Sylvia Plath: Correspondence 1950–1963*), in 1975, she too had to have the Hugheses' permission, and they exercised strict control over which of Sylvia's letters, and which parts of letters, could be published. Strangely, a great many of Sylvia's comments praising Ted Hughes were deleted by the estate. (The Indiana University collection includes all of Sylvia's letters home, from 1950 when she went away to college through her death, as well as her mother's original manuscript of *Letters Home*, before the Hugheses' deletions were made. By comparing this manuscript version with the published book, one can see what changes were requested. There is also silent control: Mrs Plath would never have tried to publish those of her daughter's letters which were critical of her husband.)

No one can publish any part of the material collected at either Indiana University or Smith College without the written permission of the Hugheses. A tiny fraction – less than 1 per cent – of any material, published or unpublished, is considered 'fair use,' but even that small quantity may be subject to the estate's approval.

In short, the problems of writing the Plath biography became the problems of dealing with the estate. Unfortunately, the changing legal situation in the States contributed to giving Ted and Olwyn Hughes extensive power in their often unreasonable attempts to control all writing about Plath. My intentions to represent her life and work justly counted for nothing with the estate. What did count was the current state of copyright enforcement, and the changes that occurred in 1986 and 1987, when American novelist J.D. Salinger, the subject of a biography by British author Ian Hamilton, prevented that book's being published, under charge of copyright infringement. This is the chronology of legal decisions that were in play during and after that decision:

1. The 1976 Copyright Act codified the doctrine of fair use, which says that authors have a limited right to quote or paraphrase copyrighted material without the copyright owner's permission.
2. In the 1985 *Nation* vs *Time* lawsuits over *The Nation*'s publishing excerpts from Harper & Row's book on Gerald Ford's pardon of Richard Nixon, Justice Sandra Day O'Connor perhaps

unintentionally gave what was to become a troublesome version of her majority opinion, stating, 'Under ordinary circumstances, an author's right to control the first appearance of his undisseminated expression will outweigh a claim of fair use.' She went on to say, seemingly without realizing the contradiction, that assessing the fairness of any attempted use of copyrighted material 'must always be tailored to the individual case.' She had also stated, however, that the Supreme Court would not 'sanction abuse of the copyright owner's monopoly as an instrument to suppress facts.'

3. In the highly visible case concerning the Hamilton biography of Salinger, outcomes did, in effect, give copyright holders the power to suppress facts. In the cases of the Stravinsky biography by John Kobler, and David Chandler's *The Binghams of Louisville*, Macmillan – the publisher in both cases – cancelled the books rather than face suits.

4. By April of 1989, the Second Circuit judges also found in favor of the estate of L. Ron Hubbard, founder of the Church of Scientology, against Russell Miller, author of the Henry Holt biography of Hubbard who used Hubbard's unpublished letters to show how different the private person was from the public figure; here, copyrighted words were used as biographical data. An appeal to rehear the case in August of 1989 was voted down 7–5.

The Hugheses were well-informed about changes in American law, better informed than I was. I was, after all, writing a biography, and to do that I was tracking down nearly two hundred people who had known Sylvia, and interviewing many of them; re-reading all the academic work on Plath that had been published since her death; and spending long days reading the hundreds of manuscript pages of her writing, as well as correspondence, at the library collections. I traveled in England, interviewing people in both Devon and London – including Olwyn Hughes herself, and in the Boston area. And I logged hundreds of hours of telephone conversations.

And then I wrote. My system for doing accurate biography was to draft each chapter and then send the chapter to anyone who might be mentioned in it. In some cases, chapters went to more than twenty people – and many of them returned the pages with extensive comments. I was sending these draft changes to the Hugheses at the same time, and making whatever changes Olwyn seemed to think were appropriate – though I could see that whenever Ted Hughes was in the narrative, Olwyn's reactions were very protective.

And then I thought I was finished. The immense amount of material had been condensed into something over four hundred pages, and I was satisfied. I had revised and revised; but finally, response from the Hugheses was that what I had written was still inaccurate and must be changed. I did what I could, though specific points from Ted meant leaving out nearly all the personal detail from his and Sylvia's marriage, changes to which I could not agree. Then passed months of silence. The Hugheses would not answer my requests for permission to publish Sylvia's writing in the biography, nor would they give me permission to publish the book.

After more than a year of this waiting, and hearing the rumor that the Hugheses were helping a British biographer write a book on Sylvia, my American publishers decided to publish a shorter book, reducing what I had written so that the biography could appear without the Hugheses' permissions, on the basis of 'fair use.' I cut my manuscript from 425 pages to 275, leaving out nearly everything that would have required the estate's permission. In the fall of 1987 the book was published, and 17,000 copies of it were sent to bookstores – before either the Hugheses or I had received copies. The day after Olwyn Hughes received her copy of the published book, the publisher received a telex from her saying 'Request Withdraw All Copies of Plath Biography as in Breach of Copyright.' (This was 14 October 1987). By having sent the bookstore orders out in advance, the publisher kept the book from the fate of the Salinger biography.

Unable to prevent distribution in the States, on 31 October 1987, Olwyn Hughes wrote to Alison Samuel, at my British publishers, who had scheduled publication of the book for the spring of 1988. Because of her demands, the American edition of the book was changed (and shortened yet again) to remove passages and details she found 'objectionable.' (Usually, the American edition would have simply been reprinted by the British buyer.) Notice Olwyn's use of current American legal decisions in her correspondence with the British publishers. She first refers to the percent of the book which is quoted material, saying 'An injunction has just been granted in the US against the Stravinsky biography because of 3 % of quotation.' She also pointed out that I had used some paraphrase, noting, in her words, 'And then of course there is all that amateur paraphrasing (as in Salinger case).'

Once Olwyn convinced the British publishers that she understood US law (though much of this would not have affected British publication at all), her main point followed: 'Clearly until we satisfactorily agree on the final cutting I cannot give permission to quote.' The 'final cutting' was of the version of the published book being sold all over the States – and so far as my contract with the British publisher read, they were to publish the same version that had appeared in the States and Canada.

The changes Olwyn Hughes then requested ran to 140 separate sections of the already much-shortened American version. The British publisher did make some changes, some serious ones, and the Hugheses then asked that all foreign editions be based on the British edition of the book, not the American, a change in procedure that was again based on the assumed 'copyright violation.'

The issue throughout was, what kind of copyright protection should be allowed to infringe on the scholarly use of materials that may be / are necessary to arrive at, and present, the truth of situations and character. Buffeted as I was throughout the writing of the book by Olwyn Hughes' frequent 'corrections,' and here follow some samples of her input, I knew that any pressure she would apply would be for one purpose only – to make me show Sylvia Plath in the most disparaging light possible.

For instance, from early in our correspondence, 30 August 1985, following her statement to me, 'You have no idea how utterly boring all this Plath nonsense is for me,' Olwyn wrote,

> The assumption here and elsewhere is that Plath was somehow the great catch. But I know what Ted's friends have always known – as attractive man *vs* attractive woman, she is not in the same league. She was nice looking, granted, vivacious and all. Not beautiful unless maybe when sunburnt and blonded and if one admired Doris Day types. She went to Smith. But Ted went to Cambridge. And Mrs Plath was just a little teacher. My first reaction to Sylvia, and that of . . . several of his [Ted's] friends, was rather disappointed. She seemed, though turned out not to be quite this, a pretty average, nice looking, American student, bright and smiling, rather tense. Ted had had much more immediately impressive girl friends. Also her family background was modest (if one listens to Aurelia, practically bread-line).

In a similar letter, Olwyn again questioned my emphasis on Plath's publishing her work: 'just a student who wrote poems . . . you make much of her being actually published. This was surely only a few poems in magazines. Ted had published a few poems in magazines too.'

Olwyn was good at insulting both my work and myself. In one place she was evidently quite angry about my presentation of Ted, calling it 'quite amazingly rude and insolent.' Then she asked, in a kind of strange *non sequitur*, 'Would you have said all this to his face? To my face? What kind of rude imbeciles are you Americans?'

The only correspondence from Ted Hughes about the book was his 3 March 1986 cover letter to my first British editor (Andrew Motion), accompanying the fifteen pages of deletions he requested from what I had thought was the final version of the book (the 425-page version). His deletions included every mention of his family – parents, siblings, older relatives – and their backgrounds and lives; every mention of his various extramarital affairs, including the most active one with Assia Wevill, with whom he had a child; every mention of his two children with Sylvia, and their role in the couple's lives and art; and any item he thought could conceivably be labeled 'invasion of privacy.' One example of the latter is Sylvia's comment, from an unpublished section of her journals, 'Boy, when I get to be 50 and if I'm famous, there will be no tribute to "The loving husband without whose help I would never have succeeded etc. etc." Everything I have done I have done in spite of Ted and against the malicious obstacles he has, wittingly or unwittingly, put in the path of my writing.'

The tactic my British editor was taking with the Hugheses at this time (because he did want the book to come out in England, and many works about Plath have been stifled there, never to see print) was that I was a 'naïve' American academic who didn't understand the complexity of Plath's life, especially her life with Hughes. Ted replied to that gambit by agreeing. In his cover letter, he wrote, 'She [Wagner-Martin] is too naïve for the subject. She's so insensitive that she's evidently escaped the usual effects of undertaking this particular job – i.e., mental breakdown, neurotic collapse, domestic catastrophe – which in the past has saved us from several travesties of this kind being completed.' Fully aware of the results of the kind of debilitating pressure the Hugheses' responses caused various biographers, they had watched – with evident satisfaction – the ruin of the earlier Plath biographies. Happy that my book had indeed appeared in the States, and was about to come out in England, though in a still shorter version, and then to be translated into three other languages, I revelled in my 'insensitivity.' But I wondered how living with the Hugheses would have changed the outlook of even the most confident and ambitious young American woman.

Once the book was published in England, many reviews were good but others were bemused, critical of themes or details that few other readers had been troubled about. Whether the severe reviews came as a result of the Hugheses' influence with reviewers, or because the readers simply disliked the book, one cannot know. When Frank Kermode began his review for the *Sunday Telegraph* (6 March 1988) by describing me as a woman from a midwestern university who taught in that unlikely field of 'women's studies,' the review would hardly swell to an expression of triumph. Or the *Guardian* (3 April 1988) when Stuart Sutherland complained that 'Wagner-Martin deliberately concentrates on the life' – as if the nature of biography were somehow in question, I ran for the comfort of the positive American reviews. One British reviewer (Douglas Dunn), trying hard to discredit the book, wrote a long digression in the *Glasgow Herald* (5 March 1988) about my use of 'a domestic idea. Around its kitchens, bathrooms, and bedrooms moral values accrue to determine a person's worth according to rules of consumption, sanitation, and sex.' What this comment had to do with the biography I was unsure, but the critic returned to his metaphor, after allowing that because Plath had been American during the 1940s and 1950s, my describing that culture during those years 'was not altogether gratuitous,' though its effect was that of a 'background soundtrack, a cheap cultural sadness.' What he seems to be most offended about is 'the material-istic squeaks that express all those kitchens, bathrooms, and bedrooms in the nice houses where nice people live, with their tidy ambitions, neuroses, and apocalyptic foreign policies designed to keep the sprinklers turning on the summer lawns.' By the time Plath had lived three years in England, if she had not understood it all before, she had learned that all art – even book reviewing – is political.

Another pattern in the British reviews was complete inaccuracy. In various of them, Sylvia was 7, 8, 9, 10, or 'young' when her father died. She also had this very different career as a college student – she did not publish at all, she published a lot, she was a 'neurotic genius' (*Times Literary Supplement*, 29 April 1988) – or she was certifiably crazy throughout her life, as if the one summer of depression which ended in her single suicide attempt occurred every year. Critics also had dif-ficulty remembering much about her parents. In Douglas Dunn's review, Otto Plath was 21 years younger than her mother, so that when he died at 55, Aurelia would have been 76, while Sylvia was 8.

Another painful critical pattern was to emphasize the way I – although I was this poor, untalented, and naïve American academic with the dull prose style – mistreated Ted Hughes. Although I had consciously avoided the almost automatic criticism other biographers and critics had levelled against Hughes, hoping to escape the charge of being 'feminist' in my presentation of their marriage, the reading seemed automatic. One of the (London) *Sunday Times* (13 March 1988) follow-up stories was Charles Oulton's front-page item on the fact that Ted would not do housework, complete with his denial of any such stubbornness on his part. The relevance of this kind of story to my aim of evoking understanding of Sylvia Plath was as remote as many of the reviewers' considerations of the book.

It was, however, hard to separate readers' interests; they seemed to want to consider Plath and Hughes together. Ted was aware of this, as he had written the British editor at the time of his requests for changes in the earlier manuscript. He had announced early on that 'the most interesting and dramatic part of S.P.'s life is only 1/2 S.P. – the other 1/2 is me.' To that comment, I had no ready answer – except that for me, the only story that was worth telling was Sylvia's, and the way she dealt with marriage to such an immense, and obdurate, ego.

Then in 1993, more than seven years after I had finished writing the Plath biography and almost six years since it was published, Janet Malcolm's 63,000 word exploration of what writing biography of Sylvia Plath was like appeared in *The New Yorker* (23 and 30 August 1993). Although I had talked often with Malcolm in the several years of her work on this project, her essay managed to obscure most of the information that is relevant to her study. While I realize that she wanted, most of all, to write her own narrative – i.e. 'story' – about biography, there seems little reason for her to have disguised a number of pertinent issues. Rather than illustrating what she calls 'the transgressive nature of biography,' her essay/book instead shows readers what she terms 'one of journalism's uncontested privileges . . . the freedom to be cruel.' Surely, the memory of Sylvia Plath deserved better.

Most biographers go to great lengths to build the factual foundation for a narrative which they hope has the vitality of story. Game-playing with the psyche of either subject or biographer hardly advances the art of biography. The Boswellian types who enjoy their roles as biographers are usually not journalists, not media-oriented publicity hounds; to be left alone to do their work is their definition of an ideal world. Until the present quasi-adversarial attacks upon biographers subside, the excellent work literate people all hope to see written and published as biography only stands to lose.

7

Problems and Pratfalls of a Literary Biographer

RUSSELL FRASER

The writer's trade is sedentary, and when things are as they should be, the writing uses up the life. This is hard on the literary biographer, obligated to the facts, however prosaic. Take Shakespeare, prosaic and then some. Ben Jonson, soldiering in Holland, killed his man in single combat, but he kept his head down and died in his bed. Telling his story, you have to work 'on your imaginary forces,' advice he offered theater-goers. I tried to follow it in two books, *Young Shakespeare* (1988), and *Shakespeare: The Later Years* (1992).

R.P. Blackmur, our best American critic, engaged me in another biography, *A Mingled Yarn: The Life of R.P. Blackmur* (1981). Blackmur's life, almost half of it lived in the ivory tower, is even less exciting than Shakespeare's. Too young for the First World War, too old for the Second, he never soldiered either. He volunteered for duty as an Air Raid Warden, though. Of course, like Shakespeare, he lived much in the mind.

Friends of his and some enemies are still around to swap anecdotes, and for me his presence remains as lively as today. Shakespeare, on the other hand, has been dead going on four hundred years. Readers sometimes ask which biography gave more trouble, and I tell them it all depends. Shakespeare used to bristle with a decalogue of Shalt Nots, handed down by self-appointed keepers of the flame. Sanitizing the facts, they looked the other way at the unfaithful husband, absentee father, and delighted purveyor of bawdy. Most who wrote about him followed suit.

But all that was mortal of Shakespeare fell to dust a long time ago, a blessing for his biographer. No thin-skinned relatives wish he wouldn't say that, no literary executors keep watch before the portals, and friends and enemies have lost their chance to set the record straight or get their own back. Copyright, if any, having expired, acquisitive publishers don't threaten to sue. Altogether, life is easier down among the dead men.

I learned this the hard way when I wrote the biography of Blackmur. He was Richard to me, not Dick as to some, or Professor, and in his last years we were friends and colleagues at Princeton. To one junior instructor, he looked older than time, but barely made it into his sixties. Also he looked every inch the professor, natty in the tweed suits he bought from Rogers Peet. That was deceptive, possibly deceiving, for this self-taught man had never graduated from high school. Few Ph.Ds matched him in erudition, however.

When he died in 1965, I undertook to write an essay-length memoir. But the essay got beyond itself, turning into a book. It wasn't hagiography and didn't lay the hero out for viewing, all the blemishes that partly declare him smoothed away. Richard Blackmur was arrogant, could be cruel, drank too much (but which of us didn't in those days), talked too much, sometimes saying more than he knew. He was himself, however, his vices being the other side of his virtues, and the pretension, failing to diminish him, endeared him.

'Saltatory,' a word he liked, describes his habit of mind, jumping from one place to another. On the lecture circuit, he jumped from novels and poetry (Dostoevsky, Wallace Stevens) to the way we live now. The highbrow critic was a moralist, among other things. Short on cash but liking French wine and a greenhouse in winter, he gave a lot of lectures. 'A Lion Is in the Path' was his all-purpose title. It might have furnished me my title for the biography, though at first I didn't know the lions were out there. Not blocking the path, they hid in the bushes, waiting to pounce. I should have seen their tails twitching, but this is the wisdom of hindsight.

Once, when an absent friend of Richard's made a target for catty remarks around the table, he said frostily: 'I like David Daiches, I like his wife, I like his dog.' My sentiments exactly, and I thought the way to honor him was to take him all in all, not picking and choosing like the Renaissance Pope who draped breeches on Michelangelo's nudes. Many in Princeton, cherishing a plaster saint, resembled this 'Breeches Pope.' Combing through Richard's things in the days after his death, one of the devout turned up his private diaries. Blotted with fears and sorrows, they make painful reading. However, said this old crony to the novelist George Garrett, they couldn't be Richard's, not in character at all.

Some credentialed academics despised the man without credentials, others remodeled him in their own image. A well-known literary critic, imported from abroad but not traveling well, identified with the failed biographer who left the life of Henry Adams unfinished. He himself meant to write the big book on Yeats but never got round to it. This rankled, and those who ventured where he wouldn't had to pay.

Another member of the clerisy wrote a slew of books, all smelling of the lamp, though. Meanwhile the autodidact, gifted with tongues, needed only to open his mouth. Anyway, his jealous enemy thought so. Richard's friend Delmore Schwartz, proposing a masquerade where everyone was to come as one of Henry James's characters, cast him as Gilbert Osmond, the perverted esthete who got off on *objets d'art*. Pro and con alike turned thumbs down on my biography. Commenting on his troubles with the life of Adams, Richard said, 'One should write lives only of those of Virgin Birth and Virgin Families.'

Growing up poor, like Citizen Kane he became a collector. He saved personal letters, bits of string, even old phone bills. Some of his correspondents thought it 'baseness to write fair,' like the statesmen in *Hamlet,* and notes from the painter Waldo Peirce needed decoding. Peirce's writing was slapdash, Richard's elegant but cramped. Pondering long, he almost never revised, and being thrifty left no margins, left or right, top or bottom. As his reputation grew, he hired a secretary, redheaded Jane Jacobs. She typed his correspondence, more of it now, and he kept the carbons. Year by year, the Blackmur file got bigger.

The detritus of a lifetime, it survives in Rare Book Rooms. Princeton, where English faculty advised their students not to take his courses, has the largest collection. Other papers are housed in New Haven, Cambridge (Mass.), Chicago, etc. Custodians might think about the mixed bag they make room for, combustible enough to burn down the house. A biographer has to sort through it all. This was a different kind of lion in the path, not the labor, the torment.

I meant to call my book 'A Hero's Life,' and though the publisher said no, the title suggests how I stood in relation to my subject. If in your childhood you hero-worship Napoleon – I did, cutting my teeth on Emil Ludwig's biography – coping with his decline and fall isn't easy. You tend to write your own life, when you write someone else's. Yvor Winters said Richard did that in the life of Adams, and getting deeper into Shakespeare, I began to dream about him, even supposing I had written the plays. This last bit I kept to myself.

Turning pages in Richard's diaries, I felt the distance narrow between him and me. Sometimes he pressed me hard. The writer of the diaries lived on intimate terms with despair. Though that didn't preclude humor, it wasn't comic relief but the Yankee variety, often coarse. Leon Edel, whose career Richard jumpstarted, bringing him to Princeton to give an early Gauss Seminar, thought he meant to destroy the diaries but death took him first. I think he left them behind on purpose, intending an apologia for other eyes than his own.

The miseries he brooded on, helping define him, were the Cross he had to bear. He wasn't neurotic, an impertinent word, or his neuroses weren't open to cure. 'He was a man, take him for all in all.' As if you could efface what you were, he said scornfully. As if you wanted to!

All one summer, I biked in each day to the Firestone Library, Princeton. My marriage was breaking up, and I lived in bachelor quarters at the Institute for Advanced Study. Retrieved from Richard's dustbin, his wife Helen's letters waited for me in the Rare Book Room. Harrowing, like the farmer's sharp-toothed harrow, they said how it was when his marriage was failing. A day spent in the Blackmurs' company needed strong drink at the end.

Robert Penn Warren said Richard's one ambition was to be a real poet, but the poetry stopped in midlife and he never talked about it. It seems important to say, though, that he wrote a dozen permanent poems. Also he wrote novels, short stories, and plays. While he lived, the poetry still hung on in anthologies – Oscar Williams' *Little Treasury* was one – but his fiction, young man's work, remained a secret even to friends. So much of him he kept under the bed, both in pride and mortification.

In one of the plays, 'a mad nasty thing about Lindbergh' (his collaborator, Lincoln Kirsten, described it), he called the hero Commander Fraser. That was how he used to greet me, but I didn't know why until I read the manuscript, years after his death. It wasn't cheerful reading. As Blackmur-Kirsten see him, Lucky Lindy runs out of luck or hadn't any to start with. 'My heart's hope is my soul's despair,' Richard wrote in the poetry, and the buried life bears out the quotation.

His lecture notes are part of the life, and show you how the private and public man come together. 'Notes' doesn't do them justice. Verging on fully fledged lectures, they evoke a conscientious teacher who suffered from stage fright. Like a jazz soloist's, his best was improvisation, however, and mostly the notes function as a taking-off point. Where they took him was a wonder. Lecturing on Shaw's *Heartbreak House*, he worked his way round to Senator George of Georgia – 'he dead,' Richard said, like Mistuh Kurtz in Conrad's story – also Thomas Love Peacock. This interesting novelist wasn't everyone's possession.

'Great' teachers are spellbinders, convention agrees, and nobody compared Richard to Buzzer Hall at Princeton or Billy Phelps at Yale. But his students knew themselves in the presence of a mind turning over. It wasn't always clear, though, where the profundities left off, giving way to something different. In Rome of the late empire, he saw a correlation between the rise in the price of bread and the poor verses of Venantius Fortunatus. The critic Stanley Edgar Hyman, wowed by his learning, remarked Richard's apparent fluency in Greek, Latin, Italian, and French. Lecturing, he held a king-sized cigaret between the third and fourth fingers. Students watched, fascinated, as it burned down to ash.

Not long before he died, I sailed for Europe on the 'Vulcania' – the world it embodied doesn't exist anymore – and the first night out, wrote an exultant letter to the friend who knew best how to read it. Smoking on the aft deck beneath a string of colored lights, I held my pen in one hand, in the other a cigaret between the third and fourth fingers. Behind the fantail the moon rose and ducked like an apple on a string. Always we had poetry in common, and I quoted an old poet on 'the glories of our blood and state.' Shadows, he said they were, insubstantial.

But this could hardly be. More keenly than most, Richard heard the 'Sic transit' music. At his highest pitch, he was exhilarated, though, and he waved off my melancholy poet. 'The glories of our blood and state', he told me, 'are not shadows but substantial things.' That was the spell he cast.

It is going on thirty years since his death, time for his truth to rise again. But the dead, like the living, are casualties of fashion. His New Critical method, sanctioning double meanings, has yielded to deconstruction, whose infinite meanings reduce life to a babel of sounds. Even Shakespeare's image is spottier than it used to be. Long the doubtful beneficiary of received opinion, he has seen it eroded in our multicultural age. Revisionists have had their way with him, and yesterday's Bard is today's Black Man's Burden.

Not hero-friendly, our age likes its Shakespeare on the sinister side, 'white, Eurocentric, and male.' Generally the male is A.C./ D.C., his one redeeming feature, also meeting the taste of the time. Anticipating this taste, Oscar Wilde spoofed it too. He wanted Shakespeare gay, so invented Willie Hughes, a boy actor. 'You must believe in Willie Hughes,' he said. 'I almost do myself.' Moderns are more earnest than Oscar.

A thesis, like a picture frame, helps them manage outsize Shakespeare, and writing about him, they tend to favor a colon in the title. The plays say he liked women (Rosalind, Beatrice, Viola, others). Once at least he thought how it would be to dress up in a woman's clothes. His Mark Antony does that. This matter-of-fact begets today's fixated man. You run into him often in the alphabet journals, under headings like ' . . . Cross-dressing, Sexual Identity, and the Role of Gender in.' Academic critics can't get too much of this, ditto the reviewers who pass on foundation grants. Portraits that aim to give you the man 'in his habit as he lived' leave them cold.

Shakespeare the faux classic differs only in particulars from Edwardian Shakespeare, a good family man and pillar of the Anglican Church. But raising eyebrows, he makes better copy. The mirror image of convention's familiar icon, he builds his fortune on the backs of the poor, and wills us to believe that the man is the head of the woman. A super patriot and racist, he doesn't like foreigners, especially colored. Desdemona sees Othello's true visage 'in his mind', not him. Previewing the colonialists just then coming on the scene, his surrogate Prospero takes over the Garden of Eden. New historiographers hear nice Caliban telling him off: 'This island's mine,' etc.

A great deal of fact illuminates Shakespeare's story – E.K. Chambers, his best scholar, milked it for two big volumes – and among his fellow playwrights, only Jonson has a fatter dossier. But the fact is cut-and-dried, like a newspaper obit. The biographer's job is to say what it means. The teacher's is different, occupied with the text. In my case, the text was Shakespeare, the business and pleasure of a lifetime.

Biographer and teacher have their points in common, both aiming to make the dry bones quicken. Taking note, William Jovanovich raised a question. (He ran Harcourt Brace Jovanovich while it was still a major player on the book scene.) Himself a man of letters and good for the life of books, Mr J. as I called him was hands-on with his authors. He had published my life of Blackmur, also *The Three Romes* (1985), travel writing plus other things, and wondered what I meant to do next. I had a few ideas, the best an Around-the-World-on-Five-Hundred-Dollars-a-Day book, but none grabbed me, him either. 'Why not write the life of Shakespeare straight from the heart,' he said, 'forgetting about the scholars and their 3 by 5 cards?' So the biography in its first incarnation came down from on high, like words of the Paraclete.

Though the Pope is blessed with charismatic truth, a literary biographer's is earned. Writing from the heart, he doesn't write truth but fiction. 'My' Shakespeare meant the work, however, not the man behind it. In my deepest place, I was and still am a New Critic. I used to smoke a pipe but don't trust writers who do, and the amiable chit-chat you get in old-fashioned 'sa vie et son oeuvre' books makes me cringe. This kind of writing cares less about the text than the context. You still find it in some Marxist and feminist polemics, minus the amiability.

For the fathers of New Criticism, the author never cut much of a figure. On a hostile view, he/she was the baby they threw out with the bathwater. In a letter of the early Thirties, Edmund Wilson reproved young Blackmur, a formalist to his fingertips, for throwing out the baby. Wilson is among our most powerful critics but not the literary kind, and rarely closes with the books that engage him. The New Critical approach, more single-minded than his, gives the art first place. This is just right for practical criticism, not for biography, however. It took me a while to see that.

Closing up the books as my publisher recommended, I wrote part of a first chapter with the Holy Ghost at my elbow. Henri Pirenne wrote his History of Europe as a POW in the First World War, far from the Bibliothèque Nationale, and I took him for my model. Shakespeare was all there before I got started. He resembled Flaubert, only raised to the nth power, or the artist as Steven Dedalus saw him. Or rather, as he didn't see him. Like the God of the Creation, he hid himself 'within or behind or beyond or above his handiwork, invisible, refined out of existence, indifferent, paring his fingernails.'

I imagined a scenario, bumptious readers wanting to know what Shakespeare thought, and me rejoining that they hadn't any business asking. Opinions weren't for the Bard, who soaked up the world like litmus paper but left no pH to say how it struck him. Not being a famous author, I wrote 'on spec.' Mr. J apologized for this, but it goes without saying that I counted on his approval. Then – surprise, surprise – he rejected my biography, first version. 'You can't write the life of a man who has no existence,' he told me.

Humbled, I might have quit, but rejection made me look twice at my ho-hum view of the 'unseen good old man' behind the arras. (In *Hamlet*, this is how they speak of Polonius, a type of the artist with his hands on all the ropes.) What was he like and did it make any difference? It turned out that my questions had answers, sometimes contradictory. They weren't written in the heart, though.

The closer I got to Shakespeare (via the facts, not intuition), the more it seemed that he read nothing but trash. This dismayed his intellectual-izing contemporaries, and Jonson, with a pair of honorary degrees to his credit, was always nagging at him. But he got his pleasure from turning sows' ears into silk purses. In *Hamlet*, for instance. The story of the melancholy Dane went back a long way, and a lurid 'revenge tragedy' starring this hero was already on the boards when Shakespeare came up to London. No melodrama more simpleminded. Under the surface, though, he detected the thing of great price. To estimate the latter, you will want to know about the former, and this is where scholarship has its uses.

The Hamlet of Shakespeare's source is a blood-boltered hero, 'o'ersized with coagulate gore.' He had his ethos all right, an eye for an eye and a tooth for a tooth, also his watchword: 'Hamlet, revenge!' Theater-goers and other playwrights cheered this figment of sick fantasy, and many of Shakespeare's critics believe that Shakespeare's Hamlet is like him. If he isn't, he's a coward and/or thinks too much. In Act I, however, he doesn't think too much, he hardly thinks at all. Later, this changes, the reason he becomes our hero.

Black Othello is our hero too, different in all but color from the savage of Shakespeare's source, a brutal tale of miscegenation. Before you pronounce on Shakespeare the racist (or male chauvinist or anti-Semite), you will want to measure the distance between him and the often predictable writers he takes for his point of departure. Source study, sometimes a pedant's refuge, sometimes puts you in touch with the artist in his workshop. Doing the biography – not the same as the impressionistic essay I began with – made this possibility vivid.

Then there is Shylock, certainly a villain, despite sentimental directors. Not that Shakespeare knew all that much about Jews. Harried for centuries, they were thin on the ground in his England, and more than likely he never met one. But he saw a piece of Shylock in the mirror. Taking 'a breed for barren metal,' he himself made money by lending out money at interest. If it wasn't forthcoming on the appointed day, he went to court to get it. This doesn't acquit the villain but complicates our understanding of his story.

Acquisitive Shakespeare was libidinous too, and knew his wife carnally before they got married. Licensed to abridge the bans – unless dispensed, they were read out in church on three successive Sundays before the wedding itself – he became a father for the first time six months later. Probably his own father couldn't read or write. John Shakespeare's signature survives, more exactly, his mark, a pair of compasses, useful in his glover's trade, or the glover's stitching clamp, a 'donkey.' It has to be admitted that Shakespeare's pedigree lacks glamor. Anti-Stratfordians deplore this. Snobbish to the core, they dearly love a lord, conspicuously absent in 'the butcher boy of Stratford.' Their Shakespeare, a.k.a. the Earl of Oxford (or Rutland, Salisbury, Southampton, or Derby), tuning up at the university, refined what he learned there at Court. Cued by modern artists like Andy Warhol or Salvador Dali, he flaunted 'personality.' This improves on the impersonal playwright and poet. You can read about him in the slick-paper magazines, out of patience with the facts, though eager to accommodate gossip.

Detective novelists and true-life romancers put a shine on the apple, but the literary biographer isn't allowed to do that. What looks like constraint is liberating, though, and the facts, if you let them speak, have something to say. Applied to Shakespeare, they say that the career belongs to the talents. A box-office draw in his own time, none bigger, he attracted a lot of notice. While he still lived, contemporaries, close to half a hundred, jotted down their impressions. The Shakespeare they remember worked over his plays like a blacksmith, striking a 'second heat upon the Muses' anvil.' He may have gone to Stratford's grammar school but he didn't go to Oxbridge or sit with Bacon in the House of Lords.

Late in the 1590s, he joined a syndicate of friends and colleagues, speculators who built the Globe Theater. On one side, the men of the syndicate were businessmen out to make money. This description fits Shakespeare. A few years later, speculating again, he helped acquire Blackfriars, a private theater on the other shore of the Thames. His risk capital brought in handsome returns, and he and his fellows got 'more in one winter . . . by a thousand pounds than they were used to get on the Bankside.' Taking chances, he (1) lined his pockets, (2) realized his genius. The same kind of man wrote the plays.

He liked solving problems, but the process delighted him more than the product. When the work was done, he moved on without fuss to something else. After the Globe Theater, Blackfriars; after the tragedies, the late romances. In the poem by Robert Frost you glimpse his likeness, the woodcutter who leaves his woodpile in the frozen swamp to warm it 'with the slow smokeless burning of decay.' King Lear is his greatest tragedy, but looking at it again, he wondered if he couldn't bring off a different ending. Evidently he could, and the answer to the question outlives him. He didn't revise, however, no matter what they tell you. Recycling the same materials, he wrote The Tempest.

Not shortchanging himself, he knew that his plays and poems were much beyond the common run. (You hear him on this topic in the Sonnets.) But the best in that kind were shadows. Not taking the trouble to proofread the plays, he didn't bother to publish them either. Only half of what he wrote appeared in his lifetime, and what did was no thanks to him. The other half, waiting on his death, needed the devoted attention of friends. Otherwise, it would have perished. I can't find that he cared, one way or another.

His father John, sometime mayor of Stratford, came a cropper financially, and partly Shakespeare's career was reparations. He had to give the lie to the proverb, Like father, like son. But partly he felt obligated to report 'on the nature of things.' The phrase – a Latin poet's – is too grand for him, however, and the facts support a lower-key description. My revised description says he cared about his art, but only 'so long as men can read or eyes can see.' Meanwhile, he made plays the way Bach made music, for the glory of God, incidentally his own, and the innocent pleasure of man.

8

The Red Room:
Stephen Crane and Me

LINDA H. DAVIS

It begins in any number of ways: as a faint stirring of the senses, an alertness at meeting someone attractive and new. Biographers sometimes describe it as a feeling of being tapped on the shoulder – as though one is called or chosen to write the life of another person. For me, the call to write a biography of Stephen Crane came when I wasn't looking for a subject. I happened to read a Crane story, and I saw myself in it – saw, in fact, my lifelong obsession in it. It turned out to be an obsession I shared with Stephen Crane.

When Stephen Crane decided to color everything in his writing room red, his friend Mark Barr, who knew something about chemicals, 'gave "scientific" reasons, determined by Charcot, to dissuade him.' But Crane (who had never had much use for doctors or for science) would not be dissuaded. The walls, ceiling – even the carpeting – were colored a startling red – 'bright scarlet,' said Barr.[1]

This was in 1899 or 1900, at Brede Place, an ancient English manor house Crane was renting in East Sussex, England. Red was Crane's color. He loved red – red flames and red firelight, red leaves, red suns, red dresses, red neckties, red-headed women. (The lady of his house herself had natural red-gold hair that some people thought was dyed.) He used the color amply in his writing; most memorably, of course, in the title of *The Red Badge of Courage*, the remarkable Civil War novel published in 1895 that had made him world famous at twenty-four. He wanted red all around him.

Pegged as a war writer after *The Red Badge of Courage* appeared in 1895 (it had been serialized, in butchered form, in the *Philadelphia Press*, the *New York Press,* and other newspapers in 1894), he had written war stories and war dispatches until he was heartily sick of the subject. 'Hang all war-stories,'[2] he grumbled as early as 1896. He had done better work than 'the accursed Red Badge,'[3] as he called it: in his powerful novella, *The Monster*, and in some of the finest short stories anyone had written – 'The Blue Hotel', 'The Bride Comes to Yellow Sky', 'The Open Boat' (based on Crane's true adventure after a shipwreck when he and three other men survived thirty hours in shark-infested waters off the coast of Florida, in a ten-foot dinghy), and, in 1899, in 'The Upturned Face.'

Written in spare, taut prose – a pared-down style that bears little resemblance to the adjective-laden writing that had made Crane famous – 'The Upturned Face' concerns the burial of a soldier in wartime. It derives its tension from the 'chalk-blue' face of the corpse that is exposed to view throughout the proceeding, unsettling the soldiers engaged in burying him. It is a stunning story, tapping the fundamental human fear of death.

That Crane could turn out a near-perfect short story at a time when he was sick (he was suffering from tuberculosis) and frantically engaged in hackwork to pay his debts – writing a bad novel, *The O'Ruddy*, which he knew was bad; overseeing a lifeless series called Great Battles of the World, which Kate Lyons, the common-law wife of the late American writer Harold Frederic, was researching and actually writing – was a kind of miracle. 'The Upturned Face,' which would have been cause for celebration at any time in his career, appeared as a lone rose blooming in a garden of weeds.

In the red room at Brede Place, Stephen Crane sat in near stillness at a long writing table illuminated by an oversized lamp with an incongruous, frilly taffeta shade, writing against time, slowly writing words on foolscap. Though he was only twenty-eight – 'the boy,' 'the marvellous boy,'[4] his writer friends called him – Stephen Crane, in 1899, had already passed the peak of his fame. He wore this fame heavily. His wonderful large eyes – deep set and gray blue, like the sea – were shadowed; creases were already etched around his mouth, which was half-hidden by a scraggly saloon moustache. He was a picture of ruined beauty: handsome, classical features – finely arched brows that a woman might envy; an aquiline nose, and full lips behind the overgrown moustache – but thin and tired looking, with very bad teeth. His soft, tawny hair was not tousled but limp; his pale skin, yellowish. (It had always been yellow.) He'd been 'feeling vile'[5] since the summer, when he was sent home from a correspondent's assignment in the Spanish-American War with a mysterious high fever. In a rare admission of ill health, he wrote a friend that 'the clockwork is jiggling badly.' 'It is all up with me,' he told another.[6]

'The Upturned Face' was an understandable choice from a dying writer – a burial tale. And a burial tale set in a war, bringing the author of *The Red Badge of Courage* full circle. But Crane's obsession – if that is the right word for it – with death and disfigurement, his predilection for fires and fire imagery – had informed much of his work. The imagery ran through his stories, novels, and reporting pieces like certain glittering threads in a tapestry. They were typically associated with war – the upturned faces of dead and mangled soldiers, men with staring, 'liquid-like eyes,' and 'corpse-hued' skin, a landscape filled with burning flowers, campfires that looked like red eyes; demons, fire imps, crimson oaths, and roars.

Writing a war tale after his stint as a correspondent in the Spanish–American War, Crane described an encounter with 'a red-headed Spanish corpse. I wonder how many hundreds were cognizant of this red-headed Spanish corpse?' he wrote in the piece 'War Memories.' 'It arose to the dignity of a landmark. There were many corpses, but only one with a red head. This red head. He was always there. Each time I approached that part of the field I prayed that I might find that he had been buried. But he was always there – red headed.' (The refrain echoed an explanation that Crane had once given to a reporter who wanted to know why he had testified against a New York City police officer on behalf of a prostitute, Dora Clark, whom Crane had seen wrongly accused of soliciting. '"Why," he said, "she was really handsome, you know, and she had hair – red hair – dark red."'[7])

Crane's great fire story is his 1897 novella *The Monster*. A tale about the social ostracism of an unspeakably disfigured man and the doctor who saved his life, *The Monster*, at its deepest level, works on us as 'The Upturned Face' does, addressing the human fear of death and bodily decay. Henry Johnson, an attractive young black hostler who works for a Dr Trescott in upstate New York, saves the life of Trescott's young son, Jimmie, in a house fire, while the doctor is away. Dr Trescott then does all he can to save Henry, who has been burned nearly to death. Against all odds, Henry lives – but as a monster, his face literally burned away. At first, the fictional town of Whilomville makes Henry a hero for saving the life of a child; then, when he doesn't die as expected, he is shunned, and the doctor finds himself without patients, and his wife is snubbed by the local ladies. The story ends with Dr Trescott bleakly counting his wife's unused teacups on her 'at home' day.

'He now had no face' – this is how Crane describes Henry Johnson's injuries. 'It was simply a thing, a dreadful thing,' he writes, refraining from graphic description. We watch as people run from the monster in horror – as an obese black woman scales a fence in terror; as a little girl, catching sight of him at a window during her birthday party (a wickedly comic bogeyman scene), suffers a nervous collapse – and we listen in on the townspeople's conversations. ('They say he is the most terrible thing in the world. Young Johnnie Bernard – that drives the grocery wagon – saw him up at Alex Williams's shanty, and he says he couldn't eat anything for two days.') We are left to imagine what the monster looks like and the horror is the more terrible because of Crane's restraint.

For me, reading *The Monster* was profoundly unnerving. I myself survived a fire in childhood. I was rescued, as Jimmie Trescott was, though far less dramatically, and escaped physical injury. But my twenty-nine-year-old father – who had tried to save me, and failed – was burned to death. For many years I was haunted by the image of what my handsome young father must have looked like after the fire – particularly by what had happened to his face. In my dreams he would appear as a bandaged figure, mummy-like; or he would be standing with his back to me, or sitting in a black-dark room. Henry Johnson sits impassively and alone on a box behind the Trescott's stable, his shoulders hunched, his head 'swathed' in a 'heavy crepe veil,' Crane writes. Even the touching illustration that accompanied the story in its *Harper's New Monthly Magazine* publication in 1898 – showing Henry Johnson sitting quietly in the shadow of the stable, his hands lying flat on his knees, his head draped in a long black cloth – evoked my dream father. As in Crane's story, my father had no face. Crane had written my nightmare.

Instead of a writing table illuminated by a large Victorian lamp with an incongruous taffeta shade, imagine a young girl's dresser, painted white. On top of it is a poodle lamp with a frilly shade, of the kind popular in the 1950s. And instead of East Sussex, in Victorian England, we are in Fort Rucker, Alabama, 1961.

It is a warm afternoon in early March, and a small group of children has gathered on a dirt hill overlooking the charred husk of a house, an A-frame, wood-and-brick ranch that had burned down three days earlier. From the air, the houses on this street all look the same, like the cutouts children make from a single, folded sheet of paper. The children on the hill can see that the burnt house's roof has collapsed, leaving an enormous hole in the center, like a gigantic donut.

At twilight, the house will be patrolled by a guard, the white MP band on his helmet the only source of light in the immense darkness.

Now, in daylight, it is simply roped off to warn people away, but the children keep to the hill, way beyond the rope, as though the debris is radioactive.

From the little hill you can see that a part of the bearing wall along the back of the house has crumbled, exposing a child's bedroom. The unmade twin bed is on the right, opposite the door; the half-opened closet reveals a neat row of girls' dresses, the color of ashes. Everything in the room is shadowed, as though an unseen hand has smudged the picture with a charcoal pencil.

On the bare hill, the children sniff the still, summery air and catch a thin smoky wavelet, or think they do. In solemn tones, they discuss the fire – what caused it and who died there, though none of them knew the residents of the house or has ever been there to play. One of them – a boy, I think – says that the little girl who lived there died in the fire.

I am standing a couple of yards away, in borrowed clothes and shoes. From where I stand I can see my dresses still hanging in the closet and all my other things – all there for the taking, but I can't go in and get them.

I was eight years old. That memory has stayed with me for thirty-four years.

Until the day of the fire – 5 March 1961 – I lived in that house in Fort Rucker with my father and mother, my seven-year-old brother, Johnny, and our dog, a boxer named Bama. My father was a career army pilot, in flight school at Fort Rucker. We had been stationed there for a year or so.

The fire broke out in the middle of the night, following a party my parents had given. Apparently, Bama – who usually slept in my parents' room but had been kept out that night so that they could sleep in the next morning – barked, from somewhere in the house. The last party guests had not left until around 3.30 in the morning, and my parents had not been in bed more than a half hour or so. My father had fallen into a deep sleep. My mother woke up first, apparently awakened by the dog's barking, and she had the odd sensation that someone was watching her – as though she was in a crowded room and someone was staring at her. Then she saw smoke pouring through the crack at the top of her closed bedroom door. Without waking my father, she flew out of bed, flung open the door, and ran through the smoke-filled hall into Johnny's room, which was cater-corner to hers and Dad's, at the end of the hall.

My room was farther down, next to the den, and when my mother ran back to her room with my brother in her arms, she could see flames right next to my door and could hear me calling for her and my father. The windows were covered with heavy metal fasteners that had to be removed with tools – not the ordinary screens – but my mother's adrenaline was working, and she ripped the screen off her bedroom window and lifted Johnny out to the ground below. She told him to run across the street, wake the neighbours, and stay there – he was not to come back to our house. Then she woke my father.

I have a dim memory of one of my parents, I don't know which one, calling out to me from beyond my closed bedroom door and telling me to stay there and not to open the door – my father was coming to get me. I was so frightened I couldn't have opened the door, anyway; I could barely move.

The first thing I recall about the fire itself is waking up and smelling smoke. I was paralyzed with fear, and it seemed to take hours to get my body to move from a lying to a sitting position. When I finally did move, it was in slow motion, and noiselessly, as though the fire might hear me. I could see the dark gray crack at the bottom of my closed bedroom door, directly opposite the foot of my bed, where the smoke was coming in. I sat upright for what seemed like forever, staring at the crack under the door and waiting for my father to come in.

Directly to my left, no more than three feet from my head, was the open window. I thought how easy it would be, how quick – a lifting of the bedcovers, one step onto the floor, then three more steps across the room to raise the window and climb out. But the window might as well have been in China. I could not will my legs to move any more than if I were crippled. I knew that it was no use – I would have to wait for my father to get me out. I waited.

The next thing I remember is a man's arm reaching in through my bedroom window, straining toward me, and a voice calling me by my name and telling me to grab onto his hand. The man was Captain Dale Harbert, who lived across the street from us. He told me to keep my head down below the smoke, but I don't remember him saying that, and I don't even recall seeing any smoke, although by then it was so thick in my room, my mother was later told, that, if I'd been rescued just a couple of minutes later, it would have been too late. I must have been coughing, but I don't remember that, either. All I remember is the smell. As Captain Harbert pulled me to safety, I scraped my knee on our picnic table, which was pushed against the house, under my window. In one of my hands, I clutched a tiny good-luck doll that I always slept with under my pillow.

I was taken to the Harberts' and placed in one of their daughters' bedrooms. Their living room was soon turned into a headquarters by the firemen, and there was a lot of talk that Mrs Harbert evidently did not want me to hear. My mother and brother were across the street from me, at the home of our next-door neighbors, the Boyles. It was Mrs Jo Harbert – a young, extremely kind, motherly woman – who had the task of telling me that my father had been killed. My mother had asked her to tell me. I had repressed all memory of this scene, but a few years ago, Mrs Harbert told me about it. She had come into the bedroom where I was waiting, bringing her two daughters with her, and found me worrying about my dog and wondering where she was. When Mrs Harbert told me that my father had died in the fire, and so had Bama, the color left my face, and my expression changed completely, so that it seemed she was looking at another child's face and not mine at all.

'Not my *father*,' I said.

Later, I learned that when my mother woke my father to tell him that the house was on fire and that I was still in my room, he had tried to get down the hall to me, but the smoke was too thick. He and my mother then went into the little bathroom adjoining their bedroom, and water-soaked bath towels to cover his head. He was wearing nothing but shorts and wet towels draped over his face and head when he disappeared into the hall.

The men who came through my parents' open bedroom window and tried to get down that same hall a few minutes later – Captain Harbert and Lieutenant Boyle – found an inferno. They could not take more than a step or two before they were driven back into my parents' bedroom. The fire department had been called, and called again, but was nowhere in sight. One of the neighbors who was standing out on the sidewalk found a fire alarm on the street, but when he pulled it, he found that it was disconnected. Even General Easterbrook was there before the firemen arrived, some thirty minutes after the first call, although the base fire department was located only about a minute away. The firemen had gotten lost finding their way to the house. To get inside, they had to break down the front door with axes; they proved so incompetent – fumbling with their oxygen masks, which they had never used before, fumbling with the axes – that Captain Harbert, the gentlest of men, finally grabbed an ax from one of them and said, 'Let *me* do it.'

My father's body was found in the den, right next to my bedroom, which means that as I was sitting up in my bed, watching the door and waiting for the knob to turn, he had bypassed my room as he groped his way down the hall and had gone in the den instead. He evidently ran into the table where the telephone was, because an operator later said that she took a call from a man reporting a fire but he was cut off. He was found under a ceiling beam that must have fallen on him as he was calling for help. Bama's body was found a few feet away from his.

Two important things happened before the fire that help to explain the nature and the length of my crushing grief afterward, though what role these events played in my obsession with my father's disfigurement, I do not know.

The first happened a few days before the fire. A young girlfriend of mine, I no longer remember who, said or did something that hurt my feelings, and I began to turn her unkindness in on myself by imagining that something bad would happen to me, and then wouldn't she be sorry. I imagined that my mother or father would die. I felt very guilty for thinking such a terrible thing, but I had thought it, and I couldn't take it back.

The second event occurred on the night of the fire. My parents' party was in full swing when the time came for Johnny and me to go to bed. I was making the rounds of the company, saying good night to everyone, when my father, an incorrigible tease, kidded me in a way that I didn't think was funny. (I had no sense of humor as a child and was – as both stories illustrate – painfully thin-skinned.) He stood in the living room laughing at me, waiting for his good-night kiss. I, in a great huff, made a point of kissing one of his officer friends good night and then sailed right past him to bed. This was the last time I ever saw him.

The result of both the fantasy and the behavior – acting on the mind of an eight-year-old girl who was deeply attached to her father – was, of course, overwhelming guilt: the feeling that I had somehow willed or caused my father's death and that I was therefore being punished.

After the fire, I stood across the street and watched with the Harberts family from their carport as the covered stretcher bearing my father's body was removed from the house. And I remember wondering how that narrow cargo could be my big father. How could he fit on that thing? And shouldn't there be a second stretcher for Bama?

I do not know to what extent seeing all that was left of my father – and yet not seeing, because he was covered up – contributed to the nightmares of the faceless man that continued for decades after the fire. But my conscious mind chose to remember seeing that stretcher, while it blocked all memory of the moment when Mrs Harbert told me that my father was dead. There was a connection missed, something left unfinished; a kiss offered and declined. For years I relived that moment on the night before the fire, the last time I saw my father, and wished that I could rewrite it. If I'd gone to him then and held on to him, would the fire not have occurred? Could I have saved him? I didn't think that far. All I knew was that I wanted to fix what was broken.

It was not until I had committed myself to a biography of Stephen Crane and had begun the research in earnest that I knew much about him. Crane was obsessed with fire and disfigurement, fear and courage, and he longed for military honors. Owing to this desire, he had attended a semi-military academy near the Hudson River in New York, his sights set on West Point. (Crane's brother, William, persuaded him to pursue another course, since he believed that there would be no war in his lifetime.) Crane had wanted to be the kind of war hero my own father had been in the Korean War, from which he took away two Purple Hearts and the Bronze and Silver Stars. Stephen Crane was twenty-eight when he died; my father was twenty-nine. They both died on the fifth of a month and were strikingly similar in looks, possessing the same arched brows and similarly shaped large eyes and prominent noses. Both were ladies' men. Their personalities were similar, as well; they both had a great sense of fun. Crane attended Syracuse University; I received my BA degree from Syracuse. Crane was eight years old when his father died suddenly – the same age I was when my father died. My great-grandfather, an old-time Methodist minister who preached in the same area of New Jersey as Crane's father did, raised my grandmother on the evils of dancing and drinking, as the Reverend Jonathan Townley Crane had raised Stephen. When I was at the Newark Public Library looking at its Crane collection one year, I came across a letter from the journalist and Lincoln biographer, Ida Tarbell, saying that she had known Crane only slightly. (This was in response to a query.) Shortly after my return home, I discovered two photographs of Ida Tarbell in an antique photo album that had belonged to my maternal grandmother – one of Ida Tarbell alone and one of Ida with my great-grandfather. 'The Upturned Face' was published in *Ainslee's Magazine* on 5 March 1900 – sixty-one years to the day of the fire that killed my father. The coincidences continued to turn up – or were they coincidences? The deeper I dug into Crane, the more I found myself.

Stephen Crane also knew something about punishment. He never lived through a real fire, but he seems to have suffered from his upbringing in a way that contributed to the images of fire and disfigured bodies that haunted him, and his writing, later on.

The fourteenth child of a Methodist minister and a member of the Woman's Christian Temperance Union, Crane had been reared, from the cradle, on fanatically religious teachings – on fire-and-brimstone rantings about hell and eternal damnation – that seem to have left the bright, deeply sensitive child frightened and emotionally scarred.

Although Stephen Crane early rejected the family religion, it was in him. The fire scene in *The Monster* in which Henry Johnson is defaced is rendered as a stunning seduction scene with biblical overtones. In Dr Trescott's laboratory, which is on the ground floor of his home, chemicals have exploded, transforming the room into a kind of hellish Eden, 'like a garden in the region where might be burning flowers.' In the midst of this fire garden, Henry Johnson, who is carrying young Jimmie Trescott in his arms, encounters 'a delicate, trembling sapphire shape like a fairy lady. With a quiet smile she blocked his path and doomed him and Jimmie. Johnson shrieked, and then ducked in the manner of his race in fights. He aimed to pass under the left guard of the sapphire lady. But she was swifter than eagles, and her talons caught in him as he plunged past her.' Johnson is knocked down on his back, at the bottom of the doctor's desk. Chemicals in glass jars are shattering on the desk, and one of them contains a red liquid, a serpent in the garden, 'a ruby-red snake like thing' which oozes across the desk and down it, and consumes Henry's face. This, too, is carried out as a seductive dance.

It coiled and hesitated, and then began to swim a languorous way down the mahogany slant. At the angle it waved its sizzling molten head to and fro over the closed eyes of the man beneath it. Then, in a moment, with mystic impulse, it moved again, and the red snake flowed directly down into Johnson's upturned face.

In Stephen Crane's rich and highly original imagination, the religious rantings he had heard as a child – with their terrifying images of the lake of fire, for instance – seem to have been transfigured, to reappear in his fiction and poetry as black riders, galloping out of the sea; as upturned faces on a battlefield; as men who lose their battle with the fire god. He couldn't get it out of his head. A fifteen-hundred-word story he wrote based on a dream he had at Brede Place, called 'Manacled,' tells of an actor performing in a play with real handcuffs on his wrists and ankles, when a fire breaks out in the theatre. Everyone – both audience and cast – flees, forgetting the manacled actor on the stage, who can take steps of only four inches, one at a time. He is left to struggle off the stage and down its back stairs in his cuffs, where Crane leaves him doomed and alone to die in the fire. (Significantly, Crane dreamed the dream and wrote the story in the midst of his own slow decline from tuberculosis.) He seems to have invented a fire for an early reporting piece called 'The Fire,' in which he tried out some of the images he would use to greater effect in *The Monster*. And in a later story called 'The Veteran,' Henry Fleming, the reluctant hero of *The Red Badge of Courage*, is resurrected. Now an old man, Henry dies in a fire while rescuing some colts from a burning barn.

As a writer, Stephen Crane was a shameless recycler, using the same words and images again and again, often until he had reached the best revision, or the culmination of what he'd been saying, or trying to say, in other work. The germ of 'The Upturned Face,' for instance, was first sketched in one of Crane's War tales, 'The Price of the Harness:'

'Cover his face,' said Grierson in a low and husky voice, afterward.

'What'll I cover it with?' said Watkins.

They looked at themselves. They stood in their shirts, trousers, leggings, shoes; they had nothing.

'Oh,' said Grierson, 'here's his hat.' He brought it and laid it on the face of the dead man. They stood for a time.

It was apparent that they thought it essential and decent to say or do something. Finally Watkins said in a broken voice, 'Aw, it's a damn shame.' They moved slowly off the firing line.

In 'The Upturned Face,' the burial team recites what they can remember from the Spitzbergen burial service.

The Monster is a devastating and masterful crystallization of all Crane had been working up about fire and disfigurement; everything he'd written on these themes until then seems to have been in preparation for this short, great work. On its simplest level, *The Monster* is about alienation, the isolation of the dispossessed character in a society that rejects him. Like the writer in society, Henry Johnson starts life as someone different – a Negro. And then his singular act of courage is rewarded with more rejection, and, ultimately, with banishment, as Crane's personal courage, in writing and living according to his own beliefs, had forced him into permanent exile. *The Monster*, located in fictive Whilomville (based on Crane's childhood town of Port Jervis, New York), was written while Crane was living in England with a woman who was not his wife and feeling that he could not go home again with this pretend wife. Cora Crane, née Taylor, still legally married to a British officer, was well known to American journalists as the former proprietress of a Jacksonville, Florida, 'sporting house,' the Hotel de Dream, where Crane had met her.

After Stephen Crane experienced war firsthand as a journalist in Greece for the Hearst newspapers and in Cuba for Pulitzer's *New York World*, after he had seen friends and strangers lying shot and dead on the battlefield, 'he could not shake an obsessive imagining of what it must be like to be hit at this or that point in the body,'[8] writes the distinguished Crane scholar J.C. Levenson. And it is true that Crane's war tales and war reporting are littered with corpses, wounded men, upturned faces, and staring eyes, the distinctive Crane imagery and view exploring again and again 'the awful majesty of a man shot in the face.' Writing about a sergeant signaling under fire at Guantánamo Bay during the Spanish–American War, Crane lays bare his obsession: 'It seemed absurd to hope that he would not be hit; I only hoped that he would be hit just a little, little, in the arm, the shoulder, or the leg.'

For all Crane's irritation at editors wanting him to write about war, war, war – war, with its crimson color, fascinated him. And it was red: the bloody bandages, 'the terrible red of the man's face, which was of the quality of flame as it appears in old pictures;' a red fez on a Turkish soldier. And yet Crane's obsession with disfigurement and death had been part of him long before he saw war.

Early in *The Red Badge of Courage*, young Henry Fleming – a 'youth,' like Crane (who was twenty-one and twenty-two when he wrote the war novel), and who, like his creator, '[tries] to observe everything' – comes across a dead soldier in the woods. While the rest of the ranks move around the corpse to avoid it, Fleming is captivated by it.

> The youth looked keenly at the ashen face. The wind raised the tawny beard. It moved as if a hand were stroking it. He vaguely desired to walk around and around the body and stare; the impulse of the living to try to read in dead eyes the answer to the Question.

Was this the actual source of Crane's preoccupation with death and disfigurement, or the deeper source: his nagging worry about what the dead know, that only the dead have been to 'the undiscovered country,' which unhealthy Crane, throughout his short life, had felt to be close at hand? Stephen Crane had been a sickly child, a tubercular adult who sensed that he wouldn't live long. (It is noteworthy that the corpse Fleming sees has a 'tawny' beard – Crane's own hair color. And, as Michael Fried has noted, as if to underscore further the writer's identification with the corpse, Crane writes that the soles of the dead man's shoes 'had been worn to the thinness of writing paper.')

Death and disease had been frequent visitors to the heavily populated Crane household, marking young Stephen – the last of the Reverend and Mrs Crane's staggering brood – in ways we can only guess at, since Crane left no record of his own feelings about it. Five of his brothers and sisters had died before he was born. His father died suddenly when Stephen was eight; his beloved sister Agnes – the sibling most like him, who was also his first literary mentor and his surrogate mother – died when he was twelve. His brother Luther was killed in a gruesome accident when Stephen was fourteen. (A flagman for the Erie Railroad, cheerful, twenty-three-year-old Luther fell in front of an oncoming train. His left arm and leg were mutilated, two fingers were severed, and he died of shock – not instantly but almost twenty-four hours later, a death that raises additional questions about Crane's interest in disfigurement.) Stephen's mother, to whom he was close, died after his one semester at Syracuse, his last fling with college, when he was twenty. Other family members had died as well: a sister-in-law (of Bright's disease), a niece, and a nephew. And Stephen wrote about corpses.

Stephen Crane made his name on a book about fear and its companion, courage. As a man, he was always testing these words – wading deep into New Jersey's Raritan River as a little boy before he had learned to swim, gasping as he started to go under, but keeping at it until a brother pulled him out; pulling a loaded revolver on a group of hazing fraternity boys at Lafayette College and then fainting; taking on the New York police force and its commissioner Theodore Roosevelt by testifying in court on behalf of Dora Clark; calmly rolling a cigaret while bullets ripped the air around him in Cuba. He smoked heavily, ate poorly, and generally neglected his health. He challenged Fate.

Stephen Crane died young and troubled, overwhelmed with debt and increasingly forced to turn to hackwork to stay one step ahead of his creditors, living in exile in England with a woman he tried to pass off as his wife. Cora Crane was not, the evidence suggests, the love of Crane's life, but she adored him, and he seems to have found a kind of married contentment with her. His demons never left him; he was too young, he hadn't had time enough to make peace with them, to grow up.

That his mind was tormented as he lay dying of tuberculosis at the Villa Eberhardt in Badenweiler, Germany, is heartbreakingly chronicled by Cora Crane in a letter she wrote: 'My husbands [sic] brain is never at rest. He lives over everything in dreams & talks aloud constantly. It is too awful to hear him try to change places in the "open boat!"'9 Crane hadn't had time enough to fix what was broken – to the extent that the traumas of childhood can ever be fixed. At the end of 'The Upturned Face,' the burial team finds that it has forgotten to turn the dead soldier's body over. The last thing to be covered with dirt is the face.

Even after the nightmares of my father stopped, after I had had time and help in fixing what was broken, there was no dream resolution: I never saw the horror of his hidden face. But about a year ago, as I started to write my biography of Stephen Crane, I had another dream, only this time it was a waking dream – a flashback. I was in the kitchen of the ranch house in Fort Rucker, and my father was standing at the counter with his back to me, making one of his special pizzas from a Chef Boyardee mix and adding the pepperoni he'd bought from the butcher. Suddenly he began to turn around – he was saying something to me – and from the perspective of an eight-year-old child looking *up* at an adult, I saw his face. He was smiling, that wide-grinned smile composed of straight, very white teeth, and his face was young, unlined and handsome.

9

Discovering Kingsley Amis*
DALE SALWAK

My discovery of Kingsley Amis began in 1967, when as an under-graduate I read and reported on his first published novel, *Lucky Jim*, in the context of the so-called 'Angry Young Men' movement of the 1950s. Some of the points I made then became part of my 1974 doctoral dissertation, 'Kingsley Amis: Writer as Moralist.' In 1975, *Contemporary Literature* published my first interview with Amis, and three years later G.K. Hall released my annotated bibliography of secondary writings on him. That book, I thought at the time, closed my work on the man. I would move on to other projects.

I did move on to other projects, but the subject wouldn't let me rest. A recurring edginess and anxiety visited me whenever I glanced at my Amis collection or read a new novel of his, not to mention the familiar 'tapping on the shoulder' that biographers often experience. In 1980, I re-visited Amis and his second wife, the novelist Elizabeth Jane Howard, at their Hampstead home for a follow-up interview on the occasion of the publication of his fifteenth novel, *Russian Hide-and-Seek*. Its subject – a futuristic dream world turned nightmare – seemed at the time a far cry from the apparently contented domestic life that the Amises enjoyed. But in 1982 during another visit I was surprised to learn that after seventeen years of an often stormy marriage he and Jane had painfully separated, that Amis was now living with his first wife and her third husband in Kentish Town, and that for the first time in his professional career, he had abandoned a novel in progress. Listening to him talk, I found myself wondering whether Amis would ever write a good novel again, a question that he may well have been asking himself. His confidence was understandably at a low ebb.

*This essay is adapted from a version presented at the 1991 Modern Language Association annual convention.

Every novel Amis has written reflects in some way the particular life he was leading at the time. Usually, the book can be traced back to some key idea, to some intense emotional need, to what Leon Edel calls some 'state of disequilibrium' in his being, to what Catherine Bowen terms 'some ghost within that struggles for release.'[1]It is not surprising, then, that two years after Jane had left, the idea for *Stanley and the Women* drifted into Amis's head. 'One moment I knew nothing,' he said; 'the next I knew it would be about a man with a mad son who breaks up his marriage.'[2] On the subjects of madness and the battle between the sexes, Amis has had much to say in earlier novels, but never so provocatively as in this dark comedy. With the exception of *Lucky Jim* (and 27 years later, his *Memoirs*), nothing in Amis's career would provide such an unprecedented outpouring of intense reaction among readers as that novel. As one reviewer accurately predicted, *Stanley and the Women* would be 'greatly relished and deeply resented.'[3] It took a full year of rejections before an American publisher would accept it. When Amis told me in 1985 that an English writer had approached him about writing a book on his life and work, I said with interest and alarm, 'Well, there'll be two then – one by an American.' I was committed.

Operating on the principle that if we dig far enough into a writer's fiction, we can find the real person behind the authorial voice, I spent the next three years on nothing but published sources: Amis's novels, poetry, essays, and interviews. Every word of an author's work inevitably says something about the kind of person he is. At the same time, it would be naïve to assume a one-for-one likeness between himself and his characters, or between incidents and certain events in his life. I worked hard to avoid falling into that trap, and tried to allow for the author's imagination and invention and creation at every turn. As I closely read, re-read, and evaluated everything in as broad and open-minded a way as possible, Amis's work seemed to guide me, chronologically, through his life in letters. Slowly there emerged from my study recurring attitudes toward family, friends, work, marriage, society, and his role as a writer upon which I could structure my book.

But published sources are only a start. I had to learn a great deal more. I wanted to know the personal and intellectual contexts from which the novels grew; the process by which Amis arrived at major decisions about structure, about the invention and ordering of plot, about the creation of characters. And I wanted to say more about Amis's breadth and consummate artistry in any genre that he chose to use. It was time to turn to the archives. 'If the biographer reads a writer's work carefully,' confirms Leon Edel, 'he is already in possession of a significant compass to that writer's archives, because he is made aware of the singular personality who is his subject.'[4]

While writing my book on Kingsley Amis, I was fortunate to have (with the exception of the Bodleian Library's collection of letters to Philip Larkin) unrestricted access to his archival material. Jack Gohn's 1976 bibliography alerted me to the Humanities Research Center's collection of Amis's juvenilia, his rejected Oxford thesis, and the notebooks and typescripts covering his first five published novels. Queries in *PMLA*, *The New York Times Book Review* and the *Times Literary Supplement* helped me to locate letters held at Pennsylvania State, Syracuse, Princeton, and the University of Victoria. And two colleagues led me to the Huntington Library's acquisition which includes almost one hundred drafts of Amis's novels, as well as various stories, unpublished plays, essays, notebooks, radio and television scripts along with 250 letters. Together, these materials span the entire course of Amis's career from 1934, when he was twelve years old, to 1990, and tell us much about his education, his evolution as a writer, his methods of composition, his friendships and acquaintances, and his respective tenures at Swansea, Princeton, Cambridge and Vanderbilt.

I was also fortunate to gain the early confidence of my subject as well as many of his friends and acquaintances. Between 1973 and 1990 Amis and I met in London six times for interviews, each lasting up to four hours. To insure absolute accuracy, I taped our conversations, and on two occasions sent him a transcript for correction. I handled interviews of Amis's friends and acquaintances similarly, and if I could not see an individual in person, I interviewed him or her by telephone. Beyond that, they left me completely on my own.

There are great advantages when the subject is alive, and also a great disadvantage, which is the biographer's lack of complete freedom to say what he wants about the subject. Amis's viewpoint in the preface to his *Memoirs* is of special relevance here. 'To publish an account of my own intimate, domestic, sexual experiences,' he writes, 'would hurt a number of people who have emotional claims on me, probably as much by my writing of good times as bad, and I have no desire to cause pain, or further pain, to them or myself.'[5] On very sensitive issues – his marriages, for example, or his three children – I therefore limited my material to what he or family members had said in print, or what Amis himself had told me *on* the record.

It has been said that the notebooks of an accomplished novelist offer 'a peculiar kind of biographical fact.'[6] A rebellious adolescence, a controlling father, a disappointing love, two divorces, recurring melancholy, fears of the dark, of loneliness, of possible madness, of death, and numberless other facts of personal biography may be windows on the work of an author, but notebooks can stand closer to the work than does any event. 'In the final version we have one book;' Edward Wasiolek goes on, 'in the notebooks we have the shadows of other books – his intentions, his trials, his mistakes, his uncertainties. The novel offers what he finally chose to say, but the notebooks offer us what he considered, and what he discarded.'[7]

This process is clear in Amis's notebooks for his second novel, *That Uncertain Feeling*, which avoided the 'second novel' syndrome many writers experience. Here Amis tells the story of John Lewis, age 26, who works in the library of a small southern Welsh town, making barely enough to support his wife, Jean, and their two young children in a depressingly low-rent second-floor apartment. The sub-librarianship – a fairly well-paying job – is open, and he applies for the position. His chances are improved when he meets Elizabeth, whose husband, Vernon, is very rich, very influential, and, very fortunately for John, a member of the Town Council and the Libraries Committee.

Most of the novel concerns John's entry, with Elizabeth's help, into her quasi-aristocratic world, and the degrading effect this experience has on his character. Although Elizabeth tempts him away from the sanctity of his home, a combination of moral scruples and a fear of deeper involvement compels him to repent, to renounce the position, and to move with his family to the smaller colliery town of his childhood, away from the wicked, sophisticated set of Aberdarcy. Detachment is in the long run the best escape, and John resolves 'to keep trying not to be immoral, and then to keep trying might turn into a habit.'

In Amis's notebook,[8] dated September 1952 and June 1953, we find a virtual dialogue between the author and his novel: schematic plans of major portions of the book; ruminations about technical problems; queries, judgments, opinions; and especially, reflections on his responsibilities to the reader. The latter remains a constant preoccupation throughout Amis's canon, and then as now his awareness of his reader remains paramount. In this regard Amis quotes Rossetti:

Above all ideal personalities with which the poet must learn to identify himself, there is one supremely real which is the most

imperative of all; namely, that of his reader. And the practical watch-
fulness needed for such assimilation is as much a gift and an instinct
as is the creative grasp of alien character. It is a spiritual contact
hardly conscious yet ever renewed, and which must be a part of
the very act of production.[9]

To this end Amis, in planning his novel, attends to the smallest
details. His notes tell us that the opening scene must occur in a library
'to avoid the cliché of starting the day with a man in bed.' Jean Lewis
must not come across as 'too hopeless,' for that would 'degrade the
book and alienate all sympathy' for her husband. Elizabeth will be
introduced immediately 'to get the thread started, though [there is]
no reason why the reader shouldn't be allowed to think at this stage
that an *illustration* of [the hero's] propensities is all that is meant.'
Humor must be 'kept at a minimum' and employed in chapters fifteen and sixteen only if it will 'increase the horror.' The author must
everywhere eschew malice toward his characters. 'All the behaviour
[will] be viewed as natural as possible.' Above all, there will be a moral
line to the story (hence its working title, *The Moral Man*). Even in this
early stage, the basic conflict of a man testing his moral fiber against
temptations of the flesh is clearly evident and coherently summarized.
It is a pattern that will be repeated in ensuing work: the core or
center of the conflict sketched in freehand in the notebooks.

After I completed the majority of work with the primary sources, it
was time to move out from the immediate, personal story to the per-
iphery. Reviews and essays from both my collection and Amis's
publishers' files helped me to draw on other possible readings and to
look in detail at the way that the work, once it had left Amis's hands,
had been received and interpreted. And consideration of the ever-
changing sociocultural backdrop of the twentieth century helped me
to understand better why Amis has become increasingly preoccupied
with the darker side of life. But there comes a time when a biography
has to be finished, even if its subject works on. I selected 1990 as my
cut-off date – a pivotal year, to be sure, with Amis's ascension to knight-
hood in June, the publication of his twenty-second novel, *The Folks
That Live on the Hill*, and the completion of his *Memoirs* – and in 1992
Harvester-Wheatsheaf published my study, *Kingsley Amis, Modern
Novelist*. Then, I believe, I could say that this book closed my work on
the man. It was time to move on to other projects.

The experience of writing this book has reminded me over and over
again of the importance of patience. As James Phelan writes in *Beyond*

the Tenure Track, 'More important than how soon is how well.'[10] Seventeen years is a long time to wait. In my case, it was to my advantage to wait as long as possible. I never knew ahead what a new work by Amis would be like – that is one of the joys of living contemporaneously with an accomplished writer. Perhaps, too, with the passing years I myself became better equipped to undertake this study. During some of that time I was busy with other work, and that allowed a great deal of irrelevance in my material to fall away. I threw out more than I used. From published sources to the archives to secondary materials – that progression worked well for me, but I wouldn't necessarily recommend it to someone else.

Finally, it will not come as a surprise when I say that the researching and writing of this book was not at all as organized, as straightforward, or as well-planned as my remarks suggest. In 1972 Amis wrote in a letter that in general, critics 'tend to overestimate the part played in a novelist's career by planning, forethought, purpose . . . while underestimating the role of chance, whim, laziness, excess of energy, boredom, desire to entertain oneself, wanting a change for change's sake.'[11] My experience has been that some of these words apply to the literary critic and biographer as well.

10

Spinning Straw into Gold

DIANE WOOD MIDDLEBROOK

On my 41st birthday, I received a letter from a publisher inviting me to consider writing the biography of Anne Sexton. An unusually popular poet and performer, Sexton had ended her life six years earlier, in 1974, when she climbed into the driver's seat of her old red Cougar, turned on the ignition, and, with garage doors closed, asphyxiated herself. She was 45 years old.

I knew very little else about Sexton, but much of what I knew bothered me the way publicity surrounding her suicide had bothered me. Sexton belonged to a subgroup of postwar American artists who owed their celebrity to the chaotic lives they lived, as well as to the work they produced. 'Confessional' poets such as Robert Lowell, Sylvia Plath, John Berryman, Theodore Roethke, and Sexton had made poetry seem causally connected to mental illness, alcoholism, and suicide. As a teacher, I found myself hesitating to introduce students to the work of these writers; it was often hard to see over the cultural baggage their names hauled into the classroom. Moreover, Sexton's very popularity made her an object of suspicion in academic circles. Alone among her peers, Sexton had never been to college: she held three honorary doctoral degrees but no BA.

Still, it was a good time in my life to take up a new project, and, best of all, this one had sought me out. Linda Sexton, the poet's daughter and literary executor, was offering me privileged and exclusive access to the poet's personal papers, all on the strength of a book, *Worlds into Words*, that I had written about modern poetry for the Portable Stanford series. In it, I devoted only a few pages to Anne Sexton's work, but apparently it was enough to convince both her daughter and the publisher that I was the right person for the job.

For me, however, the assignment felt like a blind date. I had never written a biography before, nor did I have a very realistic idea of how long it would take. Eleven years and many drafts later, *Anne Sexton,*

A Biography was published in 1991. And now I really know what it means to turn someone's remains into the story of a life.

Who was Anne Sexton? A suburban housewife married to a wool salesman. Sexton at age thirty suffered a mental breakdown from which she emerged as a poet. During the next fifteen years, she published eight volumes of poetry and wrote a play that was produced off-Broadway in New York. Her work appealed to a surprisingly broad range of readers, and received many awards, including the Pulitzer Prize for poetry in 1967. She became a fine performer and a shrewd businesswoman who made quite a good living off the well-funded poetry circuits of her day. Ambitious to increase the audiences for her work, she formed in 1968 a 'chamber rock' group called 'Anne Sexton and Her Kind,' and went on the road reading her poems to music. Even within academia she did well, rising to the rank of professor at Boston University, where she taught the craft of poetry.

For all the success she enjoyed, though, Sexton conducted her career in the context of a mental disorder that eluded diagnosis or cure. She attempted suicide repeatedly, was hospitalized more than twenty times, and became addicted to alcohol and pills. It was inevitable that as I delved into her life, her demons would become the focus of my life as well.

I started work on Sexton's biography in 1980, mainly by interviewing family, friends, and writers; and by poring over the large collection of Sexton's correspondence kept at the Harry Ransom Humanities Research Center at the University of Texas at Austin. The process was straightforward enough. But from the very beginning a fundamental question presented itself that no biographer, I think, ever entirely resolves: on what grounds does anyone claim the right to construct what purports to be a total view of another person's life?

Always the argument for biography rests on the assumption that some people's lives show us themes and conflicts significant to a whole cultural milieu. Sexton was such a person: a 'mad housewife' of the 1950s, a precursor of the liberated woman of the 1970s. The peculiarly widespread character of Sexton's womanly suffering, on the one hand, and her creative sublimation of that suffering in powerful and very popular works of art, on the other, were the claims to significance that made her a natural subject. Still, understanding Anne Sexton's suffering required extreme willingness to play a voyeur's role, intruding on her privacy in ways she could not have foreseen. And that raised ethical concerns.

I could take some comfort from knowing that unlike J.D. Salinger, who dragged his would-be biographer through the courts, the subject I was researching did not have a strong sense of privacy. Moreover, my subject was safely dead, and the dead, we assume, cannot take offense.

But Sexton died relatively young. And, as her poetry implies, her story is filled with addictions, sexual adventurism, and a drive to self-destruction. Some of this required partners in folly, and many of them were still alive. To protect the anonymity of certain people, I found I had to steer very widely around certain details, such as what they looked like, where they vacationed, how close they lived to Sexton's best friend. I shaved off a beard here, concealed the circumstances of an abortion there, and filled in the gaps with a mist of other details. Probably standard operating procedure for a biographer.

Then, about five years into the project, I was provided access to a resource that opened up unimagined possibilities: more than 300 audio-tapes of psychotherapy sessions. Sexton's principal psychiatrist from 1956 to 1964 had recorded their sessions for Sexton's use. Sexton agreed to these tapings because, in response to the feelings that were evoked during therapy, she often inadvertently entered into a trancelike state from which she had trouble remembering what went on. This same confusion was part of her day-to-day life as well. Especially during her husband's absences on business trips, Sexton grew desperate, often suicidal; without a trusted partner to confirm her existence, she feared she might do anything, including kill their two young children.

The therapy tapes augmented both the treatment and Sexton's sense of security. Immediately after each session, she would make notes about what she remembered; then before her next appointment she would come back to the office and play the tape, making notes. Both the poet and her doctor regarded this practice as very pro-ductive. And so it continued until 1964, when, after her doctor moved away, she entered therapy with another psychiatrist.

With the permission of both Sexton's literary executor and her doctor, I began tracking Sexton's life down this corridor of sound. And as I listened, my view of her, even as an artist, changed dramatically. I had shared the prevailing view in academia that she perhaps wasn't a 'good' poet. But on the tapes I found her abundantly forthcoming about what she was trying to do, and I learned how limited my stand-ards had been in judging the successes and the failures of her work.

Another surprise was the way my attitude toward her suicide changed. Shortly after Sexton's death, the poet Denise Levertov had written a sorrowful and moving obituary that expressed a good deal of anger at the impact Sexton's death might have on young poets, especially young women. 'I have heard many stories of attempted - and sometimes successful – suicides by young students who loved the poetry of Plath and who supposed that somehow, in order to become poets themselves, they had to act out in their own lives the events of her,' wrote Levertov. 'I don't want to see a new epidemic of the same syndrome occurring as a response to Anne Sexton's death.'[1]

I shared Levertov's dislike of the way, after Plath's death, Sexton had glamorized her own associations with suicide. But in listening to the tapes, I came to see the many ways in which Sexton's views of suicide differed from my own, and I learned a good deal more than I wanted to know about the depth of her anguish and her self-hatred – the condition she proposed to cure with suicide when therapy failed her. I came to see her self-inflicted death as an act that protected her from worse to come; I came, even, to see it as timely – an action taken with care and performed with dignity.

I spent much of two years with Sexton's voice traveling through my ears and fingers, transcribing the tapes, feeling something like the dwarf in the story 'Rumpelstiltskin' (on which Sexton had based a poem), who had the magic power of spinning straw into gold. It was a fabulous experience: as the spools of tape unwound, I heard Sexton telling her own story in her own marvelous, throaty voice, often answering directly the very questions that interested me most. Or seeming to answer – for she was an inventive storyteller, and she, too, liked the sound of her voice.

But the tapes provided far more than information; they provided intimacy. The skepticism I had brought into the project vanished as, her captive, I struggled to grasp both the manifest and the latent meanings in what she confided to her doctor and, unwittingly, to me. Such intimacy is never without costs. Invaded by Sexton's voice, I was also invaded by her pain and despair – and by the rage she cunningly triggered in her search for punishment. My respect for her psychiatrist intensified as I sat invisibly between the two of them, witnessing the resourcefulness of her pathology.

In his rueful account of his dealing with the estate of writer John Cheever, Scott Donaldson quotes a piece of advice he had received from an older and wiser biographer: 'Never write a biography of someone whose children are still alive.'[2] Fortunately, no one gave me that advice; and as it turned out, Anne Sexton's daughters became my most generous sources, first of information and then, after the manuscript was drafted, of accuracy.

When I had finished writing up the material gained from the tapes and showed the manuscript to Sexton's daughters, they reacted with outrage. They convinced me that I had gone from being Sexton's skeptic to being her apologist, greatly downplaying the terrible demands she placed on her family and everyone else who cared for her. Her daughters' angry responses to certain passages in the manuscript reminded me that they, too, had been her captives. But they hadn't been able to stop the world and get off as I had done in turning off the machine at the end of the day. Revision of this new manuscript required restoring the balance, stepping back, loosening my book from the thrall of the close-up.

Writing Sexton's biography has changed my life. It has brought me into the private lives of people I would never have known; brought me close to my subject's children in ways that make me feel like an honorary member of another family. More, it has made me a biographer, a profession of its own, different from being a professor. During the last few years that I worked on the manuscript, I found myself measuring my own progress in life by Anne Sexton's rises and falls. I remember calculating the date on which I would have outlived her by a day, and I remember that day.

But I found, at the end of it all, that she still retained a life of her own. Last spring, I was asked to read some samples of Anne Sexton's poetry at a celebratory event. I leafed through *Collected Poems* all the way to the end of the book without seeing anything suitable. I hate the end of that book: full of posthumously published writing, it shows me a Sexton wrenched by pain and alcoholism into a grotesque simulacrum of the person I had come to respect and, yes, to love. But that day I paused over a poem called 'Admonitions to a Special Person,' which I had never really taken in before; and suddenly she leapt off the page at me and asserted herself in all her sauce. Let Anne Sexton have the last word, written the last year of her life, a comment, perhaps, on her expectations of a biographer.

> Love? Be it man. Be it woman.
> It must be a wave you want to glide in on,
> give your body to it, give your laugh to it,
> give, when the gravelly sand takes you,
> your tears to the land. To love another is something
> like prayer and can't be planned, you just fall
> into its arms because your belief undoes your
>   disbelief.

11

On Being a Witness

KATHERINE RAMSLAND

On Friday, 11 November, 1994, the film, *Interview with the Vampire*, premièred all over the United States and set box office records. Anne Rice, the author of the novel on which it was based, wanted to hear the audience reactions. She invited me, as her biographer, to meet her at the Ziegfeld Theater in Manhattan. I went, just as I had flown to New Orleans the week before to join Rice in a private screening of this film for friends and family. I rode with her to the theater, sat close to her throughout the film, and attended her parties. I was the witness, the recorder of major events like this in Rice's life. I was part of it all.

When I had first decided that I wanted to write the biography of a living author, I had no idea after its publication how much I would continue to be involved with her. It makes sense, of course, but it has certainly changed my life. This kind of firsthand experience puts the biographer right in the center of things and creates a constant awareness of the need to be ready for future events. Biography is a major commitment, no matter who the subject is, and to immerse oneself so totally in someone else's point of view means merging on several levels with that person's life. With someone such as Anne Rice, who is in constant psychological evolution, the task can be daunting at times.

ANNE RICE

Most noted for her supernatural books, Rice has written five novels in the series known as *The Vampire Chronicles* and three in *Lives of the Mayfair Witches*. She has also written two historical novels, *The Feast of All Saints* and *Cry to Heaven*; a fast-paced thriller called *The Mummy*; two erotic novels under the pseudonym Anne Rampling; and, as

A.N. Roquelaure, three novels in a fairy tale setting that Rice describes as 'elegant sadomasochism where no one gets hurt.'

Raised by a devoutly Catholic mother who wanted her to be a genius but who died an alcoholic before Rice was fifteen, Rice went through a tremendous emotional upheaval early in life. Yet her creative imagination and her literary resources sustained her as she tutored herself in such great writers as Dickens, Hemingway, and Shakespeare. Tragedy came again with the death from leukemia of Rice's five year-old daughter, and soon thereafter, she wrote her first, *Interview with the Vampire*, published in 1976. Then came the surprising financial success of this novel, not to be matched again for nine years, then greatly surpassed thereafter.

When I first read *Interview with the Vampire*, I was impressed with the way Rice presented the human side of the vampire image. Told from the vampire's perspective, the novel chronicles the alienation of a creature that feels isolated, confused, helpless, and angry over his addiction to the constant repulsive ritual of taking human life. Rice's psychological contribution to vampire lore changed the way it was written from that moment on. By the time I read the third novel in this series, *The Queen of the Damned*, I was growing aware that this author was a literate, intelligent person who had infused genuine philosophical substance into characters that would otherwise be dismissed as mere genre images. As a philosophy professor, I recognized many of the themes from such writers as Sartre, Dickens, Kierkegaard, Camus, and Dostoevsky and I wanted to know more about this author. What was her background? What were her intentions? Did she realize how close she was to other literary traditions? It seemed to me that there was more than just a highly visual Gothic imagination at work. I wanted to read a biography of her, but none had been written. So I called Anne Rice and our conversation resulted in a proposal for my own biography, *Prism of the Night*.

THE BIOGRAPHICAL PROCESS

My first task was to choose a goal and format. The goal was to study the creative process as it manifested itself in Rice's unique background and perspective; this was my primary interest and it provided the focus for my research. Choosing a format required studying other biographies to see which approach most intrigued me. Since I had taught courses in psychobiography, that seemed the best place to begin.

Psychobiography, as I understand it, means exploring how an author's way of processing his or her experiences and influences shows up in characters, themes, symbols, and patterns of action. This approach can itself take many forms, and the one I chose had phenomenological rather than diagnostic qualities. That is, I was more interested in describing the evolution of Rice's inner world than in analyzing cause-and-effect. Where I needed to supplement my knowledge about such aspects of her life as alcoholism or being raised in New Orleans, I used outside sources. However, I paid most attention to the psychological content of her novels.

The primary process involved weaving together events from Rice's life with descriptions from her novels and short stories, locating the autobiographical resonance in the work, then using the work to provide further direction for investigating Rice's experiences. For example, the description of Marie St. Marie's first kiss in *The Feast of All Saints* seemed so authentic it had to be Rice's own experience, and she affirmed my intuition. When Rice described her friendship with a college roommate, I located more of the depth of her feelings from similar friendships involving her characters. Then I discovered that the character who most exemplified her life in New Orleans and San Francisco was Michael Curry in *The Witching Hour*, so I was able to establish a parallel that created a dialectic between the novel and Rice's psychological development. This made possible many significant discoveries, such as Rice's childhood fear of the Comus Parade at Mardi Gras and her love of Victorian architecture.

The next task involved my methods of interpretation. All biographers must eventually make decisions about the aesthetic coherence and organization of their material. Otherwise it can become excessively digressive or chaotic. Some sort of theme may come into focus to guide the way the facts are placed in context and that is what I explored. It seemed to me that Rice moved constantly between the Dickensian notion of living as a victim or hero; when her novels reinforced this idea, I utilized it for continuity but refrained from reducing her work to only this theme. Once having a theme in place, I needed to choose my psychological orientation.

My own preference for interpretation is Jungian, with an existential flavor. This means that I appreciate Carl Jung's perspective but remain atheoretical enough to respect Rice as a unique person rather than viewing her merely as the confirmation of an ideological framework. My approach was to allow her life to take form in its own way first, and then acknowledge where psychological theory made an interpretive contribution. In other words, I collected material first, then organized it with an approach that seemed appropriate to the facts, rather than collecting material with an *a priori* structure already intact. While this is a highly subjective method and difficult to teach, it gives biographical subjects room to unfold fully, with respect for who they are.

I was always aware of one of the central controversies of psycho-biography: that my own education, experience, and perspective influenced how I presented Anne Rice and whichever aspects of her story I decided to include. For example, since I was interested in philosophical influences, I may have emphasized certain areas of her education over others. And not being Catholic, I had to learn from the outside a religion in which Rice had been immersed since birth. Facts are malleable and the way they are interpreted will evolve with changing contexts; any aspect of a subject's life can be exaggerated out of proportion, minimized, ignored, or suppressed, depending on the biographer's overt or covert agenda. As long as biographers keep in mind that their work provides a *perspective* and not a definitive, omniscient statement, the task becomes manageable, and subjective intuition is allowed to play its part.

Certainly there are drawbacks to subjectivity. How I interpret Rice's work may say as much about my perspective as about her life. On the other hand, where I shared experiences with Rice's, I had advantages. I could find her emotional pulse to some degree from my own. To my mind, the strength of a biography lies in recreating moments in the subject's life that reveal the most profound psychological truths – about that person and about ourselves. This is best done if the biographer recognizes the force of his or her own presence in the process. Doing so aids another of the biographer's goals, which is to locate moments of the subject's life most vivid to that person and thus to enable readers to fully experience the subject.

My good fortune as a biographer was that Rice had remained true to her own artistic vision, despite pressure from publishers, friends, and fans to do otherwise; she wrote the novels that deeply interested her, and wrote them the way she wanted. As a result, I was able to trace the evolution of her imagination through various styles, genres, and personas. She wrote about the issues that most strongly engaged her attention, due to inner conflicts she was trying to resolve, and she expressed herself as vividly through such diverse characters as castrated opera singers, the free people of color, fairy-tale princes, witches, and precocious teenage girls as she did through vampires.

Although many critics evaluate Rice's writing style as florid and overwrought, her excessive emotional scenes are fairly authentic to her own intense responsiveness to the physical environment. She laughs hard, cries frequently, and is easily hurt by slight or misunderstanding. Her finely-tuned sensitivity, and her capacity for unwavering concentration and for attention to nuance, give her fiction a multi-sensory vividness. In many ways, her novels mirror her, and whenever two or more characters are in heated conflict, they often represent unresolved parts of herself.

Writing the biography of a living author who is at her prime is a unique experience. Parts of the process have both positive and negative aspects, but I believe the advantages far outweigh the disadvantages. Addressing both provides the fullest description of the range of problems and solutions that helped me refine my approach.

POTENTIAL PROBLEMS

Every biography has its own set of problems, but many universal issues can be gleaned from within the idiosyncratic context. As I discuss my own experience, I will note what I think can be learned for the biographical process in general.

1. With a living author, this may be the first study done, as was the case with Anne Rice. There may be no archives available, no previous scholarly perspectives, and access to personal papers may be limited (even if authorized) because the living subject wishes some things to remain private. Although being the first to write about a subject leaves the field wide open, it requires extensive fieldwork and fact-gathering, good organizational abilities, and a developed biographical instinct for making the most of the resources available. The amount of work can require years to complete.

2. On a more personal note, although mine was not an 'authorized' biography in that Rice neither chose me nor exercised control over the direction I took, she agreed to cooperate and spoke to family and friends on my behalf. Thus, my task was similar to that of an authorized biographer: to find a balance between writing an exposé that could offend her and close doors to me, and composing an accurate description of sufficient detail and depth to interest my readers. I walked a tightrope between these two poles and what I decided was this: where 'tell all' aspects contributed nothing to my goal, seemed petty, or only hurt people, I left them out, and where analysis seemed intrusive or superfluous, I avoided it. My primary

interest was to identify and describe the events and sources of inspiration in Rice's life that influenced the most profound aspects of her work, and I discovered plenty of material.

3. Which brings me to another potential disadvantage: keeping up with it all. There is an openendedness to biographies of living authors, and the constant flow of information can be overwhelming. At times, Rice says something in an interview that expands or even contradicts information I have gathered, which makes me want to rewrite my book. And whenever she releases a new book, there is such a vast flurry of media attention that it is impossible to collect everything. My biographical role often feels futile and I have to remind myself that much of the new information is merely repetition. I can only hope that I will acquire the most important elements for future revisions.

4. In addition, there is a lack of closure to such biographies that can be disquieting. For one thing, although we have made a joke of it, Rice and I are both aware that my book will not be truly finished until she dies. She must wonder whether I experience what Truman Capote felt as he waited for the subjects of his true crime novel, *In Cold Blood*, to finally be executed so he could end his book. The biographer knows that, unless he or she dies first, it is inevitable to anticipate the end of the story. Yet no one wishes the subject to die. So each time I am on the scene as a witness, Rice is aware that my continuity in her life story may require that I be the recorder of her death as well. The idea disturbs me, too.

5. Another disadvantage (which also has its positive side) is the possibility of a friendship forming. Rice appreciates my respectful approach, and in the process, has often confided in me. While I welcome such confidences, I am also aware that I have a responsibility to my readers. I do not wish to caution Rice in what she says or to violate deeply private concerns that have no business in a literary biography, yet some readers are interested in such details. The process is tricky, with no clear boundaries. The biographer can begin to feel like a voyeur. Rice and I are both aware of this. Although friendship is present, it is tempered by my scrutiny. As long as I am her biographer, I will never be fully privy to her concerns. There are times when I desire that type of relationship, yet I would not give up my professional position. The key to finding a balance lies in her trust in me, my respect for her, my ability to discern what is truly pivotal, and our mutual awareness of the inevitable conflicts in my role.

6. One difficulty I experienced was Rice's desire to be presented in

the way she perceived herself. We all tell ourselves stories about who we believe we are, for self-knowledge or ego-boosting, among other things. And since we all have blindspots, our self-perceptions are inevitably limited. These stories or personal myths become more fully developed when forced into articulation by constant media exposure. To her credit, Rice had agreed to exercise no control over my work and she understood that I was not going to be constrained by her own version of events. Thus, I was free to present her from a variety of perspectives, some of which did not agree with her own.

However, Rice had her own prerogatives. She sometimes withheld significant information, and I was (understandably) denied access to her personal diaries. I felt frustrated at times, particularly when Rice insisted in relating to me a paraphrase of the first draft of her first novel, rather than allowing me to read it for myself. I discovered later that there was a scene in this draft that revealed powerful emotions on her part, and I was terribly disappointed that they had not been included in my book (although this scene is described in a subsequent book that I wrote on Rice's novels). This aspect of writing a biography can be a power struggle, and the biographer must learn psychological skills for working sensitively with some issues.

7. I also had problems with some of Rice's friends. A few were protective, others wanted undue recognition for inspiring her, some had memories that contradicted Rice's, while the worst interviews involved acquaintances with a vendetta. These were few but they were jealous of Rice's popularity and wanted to use my book to cast a negative light on her. Not that their words were necessarily inaccurate, but the tone in which they were delivered indicated that caution was warranted. The acquaintances of a living subject often have agendas related to the very fact of the subject's awareness of them, and such motives must be carefully weighed.

8. The worst part of my experience was miscommunication. Although it was mostly a great benefit to have Rice available for comment and information, there were times when I unintentionally presented something in a way that annoyed her, and we had to rebuild our working relationship. This was not a problem when we spoke face to face or on the phone: I could usually sense from her voice if she was tired or depressed, and such were not the times to ask for long or complex responses. However, transferring our exchanges to a fax machine became tricky. Faxes can intrude at inopportune moments and thereby appear insensitive. (Yet a faxed response saves time transcribing from a tape recorder.)

THE POTENTIAL ADVANTAGES

Despite all of the above, the benefits of working with a cooperative subject who is still alive were highly rewarding and I would write about another living author for the following reasons.

1. Certainly the most obvious advantage is the ability to check the primary source for accuracy. Rice's memory of her life events is not infallible, but she and members of her family provided a continuous source of information and fact-checking. Rice was generous with her time, and asked several people close to her to look over various parts of my book so that I could get things right.

2. There is also the opportunity to experience the subject's immediacy and vitality. I saw Rice in action. Spending time with her, laughing with her, listening to her enthusiasm as she alluded to her most recent project or described a dream she had recently had, rounded out my sense of her as a writer. For example, when I first visited New Orleans, Rice took me to see the house that had inspired her description of the place where her character Lestat lay for half a century in a comatose state. And standing in her office, I was able to see one of her unique ongoing methods: she writes words she wants to use in novels all over the walls and door frames. Reading them, I could anticipate the literary directions she was about to take. She also told me what she was reading while working on a novel, which provided important sources of information.

3. The most exciting aspect of working with a living author is the shared anticipation of what may happen. For example, a Hollywood film of *Interview with the Vampire* had been in the works for eighteen years, and its history was filled with such negative twists and turns that it appeared to be cursed. Since Rice loved films and since this novel had been so emotionally cathartic for her – having been written in five weeks as she worked through grief over her daughter's death – it meant a great deal to her to get this story to the big screen. It looked as if it might never happen, so when it finally did, I became part of the experience. Rice was so pleased that I had cared enough to record the context of this novel, the history of the aborted attempts to capture it on film, and the exhilaration of seeing it completed to her satisfaction, that she invited me into every aspect of it. Fortunately, my publisher is interested in keeping the biography available and up-to-date, so that my continued witnessing of Rice's life will go into record.

4. There is also the satisfaction of correctly anticipating the direction Rice's novels will take. Having traced her psychological

development so closely through fourteen novels, I intuited a direction for her that came to pass in succeeding books. It confirmed that I was on the right track.

5. I was able to approach Rice with a 'virgin' perspective: nothing else had been done on her in a full-length book, and I appreciated the freedom that this lack of past analysis provided me. To work with a living author often means being a groundbreaker in some way. Even if other work has been done, fresh sources of information are always available. The excitement of witnessing an unpredictable or once-in-a-lifetime event in that person's life (the birth of a child, a surprising religious conversion, or a work in progress unlike anything the author has yet written) is its own reward.

6. Certainly the friendship mentioned above offers great benefits. Although I refrain from violating Rice's privacy, I am aware that being close to her offers a greater sense of who she is than if I were to remain at a professional distance. I may not write overtly about some of the things I learn, but they nevertheless inform my perspective and help me to develop an accurate assessment of the psychological dynamics of her work.

7. Writing about a living author means having a lived sense of the social and political events that may have influenced the author. Rice wrote during the sixties, witnessing first-hand much of the political turmoil and watching the rise of feminism and gay liberation. I, too, experienced much of this social upheaval and I was able to write about it with richer experiential detail than if I had merely read historical reports.

8. Working so closely with a writer who has overcome adversity and turned it into a source of creativity was personally inspiring. I learned a lot about working through grief and loss, bearing the brunt of poorly-informed criticism, living with a writer's insecurities, and finding one's way out of depression via art. I also learned many things about writing novels that will help me with my own. The biographer hopes to provide such benefits to readers, but in the process, may acquire a bit of wisdom as well.

To summarize, I needed to develop both clarity and compassion about what I wanted to understand about Anne Rice. I accomplished this by having an appreciation of (and caution about) my own subjective presence in my interpretations; a diplomatic sense of people's feelings; and a professional respect for Rice's readers and my own. I also needed to be willing to become part of Rice's world. To be a witness means not just to record what happens, but to engage with it, because living subjects are best comprehended in action. Being a receptive, flexible observer as events unfold, rather than interpreting them merely in retrospect or through a theory, is one of the richest sources for achieving a true sense of the person at the center of the biographical story.

12

Private and Public Lives

NATASHA SPENDER

In the space of two weeks, I have heard from four of my contemporaries of the stress they are under (in one case amounting to serious illness) at the prospect of impending biographies in which they will be portrayed as minor figures. These are all decent, generous, reasonable and truthful people who value privacy, and whose histories bear no relation to the public interest, since the subjects of these biographies are not politicians, public servants or tycoons, but artists, writers, musicians – people for whom Watergate-type investigations are entirely inappropriate. Though unknown to each other, in every case my friends have told me that waiting, sometimes over years, for the blow of publication to fall, and having no clue as to the use to which their evidence will be put, is an experience similar to that of being the victim of blackmail. This, because each unauthorized biographer, as self-appointed judge and jury, but acting under no restraint of the rules of evidence, sees these minor characters as mere jackpots of 'material.' He may forget that they are humans as vulnerable as himself. He asserts his right to exploit this material selectively, to present whatever picture he pleases, and in some cases dismisses any demur as to the truth or balance of his account – indeed, any request to see and comment on the manuscript before publication – as a tiresome and reprehensible attempt to obstruct his book.

Some biographers even take the attitude that if people, however helpful in interview, are 'uncooperative,' that is, unwilling to hand over to him, a total stranger, their private diaries or correspondence to use however he wishes, they must take the consequences. In a civilized country where blackmail is a crime, and where we have many distinguished biographers to whom these practices are entirely alien, it is surely time for us to re-examine the assumptions held and methods currently employed by some biographers and endorsed by some publishers. In the last decade, these have changed so drastically from formerly accepted principles that a revision of the present code of practice is urgently needed.

Certain questionable assumptions are vigorously, even self-righteously asserted by some biographers and publishers. The first is that any achievement renders a person 'fair game' for any biographical exploitation, and that the biographer is fulfilling some sort of higher duty by being 'ruthlessly disinterested' (John Lahr, *Evening Standard*, 26 September 1991). An assertion of the absolute nature of the biographer's objectivity, and of his right to stand in punitive judgment, may involve a singular lack of self-knowledge. Unlike lawyers or psychiatrists, whose years of training and varied clinical experience serve as corrective to unconscious biases, his choice of subject, and selection from the available evidence, may be unconsciously directed by his own unresolved inner conflicts or unfulfilled aspirations. The best, most scholarly biographers show an intelligent sympathy for their subjects which is truthful without being 'ruthless' (Richard Ellmann's for James Joyce, for example) and which is transparently free from such pressures. By contrast, the worst are not even unconsciously motivated, but with conscious cynicism use people's lives with little regard for either privacy or truth, presumably in order to make money.

A second assumption held by the biographer who sees himself as a disinterested historian (though often lacking the historian's training) is that the sole motivation of an artist is to promote a self-serving legend, that families and friends invariably act in bad faith to falsify history and perpetuate a myth, and therefore that their evidence should be dismissed as what John Lahr calls 'bogus sentimentality.' The artists and poets I have known well have been unconcerned with myth-making, their modest ambitions focused entirely on producing their best work. This insulting assumption ignores the fact that the friends and families who knew the biographee intimately over a lifetime possess a rich and detailed mesh of visual, auditory and verbal memory by which over many years they came to understand the consistencies, faults as well as merits, of his temperament. The biography rings untrue to them because they can immediately recall countless episodes and conversations which simply do not fit the picture presented.

By comparison, the biographer's knowledge is inevitably superficial where it is based on a couple of years' acquaintance, say, as against many decades'. The problem is even worse when the biographer did not meet the subject, cannot therefore conjure images of him, nor, if he is of a different generation, of the life and times with which long-standing friends are familiar. He relies partly on secondary sources, whereas they *know* the truth of particular events, not only as eyewitnesses but as confidantes. The present fashion of some biographers routinely to imagine there to be a 'cover-up' often betrays their failure to research scrupulously enough, or their unwillingness to forego a 'vivid' thesis if the truth does not support it. The great contemporary biographers – Holmes, Holroyd, Painter, for instance – do not see themselves as merciless arbiters, but go deeply enough to arrive at a similar, understanding consensus to that of friends, where 'tout comprendre c'est tout pardonner.'

An example of such a misplaced cavalier attitude, perhaps due to haste, was Michael Shelden's portrait, in his Orwell biography of Sonia Orwell as avaricious, uncaring both of George and of his posthumous reputation. Several friends (notably Hilary Spurling, herself a respected, honorable biographer), unhappy with Selden's mis-understanding of their testimony, wrote after publication to the *Times Literary Supplement* to correct his picture from their long experiences of Sonia's generosity, her devotion to George, her devastation at his death, and her conscientious responsibility as his literary executor, to all of which I can bear witness. Yet he dismissed their evidence in his reply (*Times Literary Supplement*, 8 November 1991) and appeared to have preferred to rely on vague gossip than on Anne Dunn's eye-witness account of the long evening of George's death which she spent in Sonia's company. Had he checked before publication with Anne Dunn and with those other informants, a more balanced, truthful picture would have been presented. Though deploring its likely perseverance in history, one may be thankful that Sonia was no longer alive to suffer from this portrait. For the living, such experiences have been described as having thereafter to face the world with a false persona imposed, like a grotesque mask plastered over one's natural face.

For families and friends, in many cases the nightmare unfolds as follows. A polite letter requesting an interview arrives, often on university writing-paper as earnest of the seriousness of the enterprise. The biographer assures them that he or she intends giving a sym-pathetic picture and emphatically is 'not a muckraker.' A dangerous signal this, since the idea is obviously in his mind. Friends may be told that he has 'the full cooperation of the family,' but it would be wise to check whether that is indeed so. (As a friend, enquiring recently of two families, I found in both cases that these claims were unfounded.)

The friends in turn feel that it is better to grant an interview to this stranger, about whose motives, intelligence and goodwill they can as yet know nothing, and whose probity they must take on trust, because their own knowledge can contribute to the truth of the book, and truth is preferable. They are often assured that they will be given an opportunity to see and comment on the chapter which concerns them, though often this promise is then withdrawn, and a picture they know to be untrue emerges. They discover that their candid account has been distorted or ignored. On the strength of their once having seen him, or even answered a single question on the telephone, he makes free to cite their names, thanking them in acknowledgements, so that the reader is erroneously led to believe that it is they who have provided 'facts' emanating from elsewhere which they know to be untrue, and have endorsed a portrait which they know to be false.

The miserable prospect of the book being accepted as objective and used as a secondary source must be endured, with the added knowledge that the hardback will be available in libraries, long after any attempts to put the record straight in ephemeral newspapers have disappeared. Neither the public nor even reviewers are equipped to judge the book's veracity from acknowledgements or citations of 'personal communication' in notes, where there is no clue to the depth, conscientiousness and selectivity of the research, nor the degree to which informants approve the result. That the self-consistency of a portrait can be the product of the biographer's inbuilt biases is particularly apparent in some feminist accounts of Virginia Woolf and Sylvia Plath, where Leonard Woolf and Ted Hughes are, to my personal knowledge of them, very unfairly misrepresented. The moving plea by Hughes (*Times Literary Supplement*, 24 April 1992), for his children to be spared the daily ordeal of facing people who will by now believe a slanted, hurtful account of both parents, should be carefully read by any biographers tempted to imagine that their theories justify closing their eyes to human suffering.

The reader cannot know that out of an hour's appreciative interview, perhaps the two half-sentences of critical comment may be the only quotations selected by the biographer. A somewhat comparable process caused pain and anger to lifelong friends and connoisseurs of Henry Moore and his work who, intending affectionate tribute to him, had in good faith given long interviews, but who later publicly protested about the untrue portrait as they saw it presented in the television biography, 'England's Henry Moore' (Letters to the Editor, *The Times*, 24 September 1988). A director may assert his right to his thesis, but had he first made it clear to them, they would have chosen not to contribute. Any request to see the manuscript and point out errors of fact may be indignantly rejected as 'censorship;' over-concentration on the prurient interest will be justified in asserting, 'I would be cheating my readers and posterity if I were not to do so.' Yet readers may be far more cheated by inaccuracies, biases, or the biographer's favoring their supposed desires for titillation as against their wishes to read a balanced and humane account. The zealous search for (and occasional invention of) clay feet is justified as 'objectivity,' when it may well be unconscious aggression. This pomposity about their *metier* tends to vary inversely with the quality of the biographer's work.

A decent revision of the code of practice would restore some of the standards observed even a decade ago, which have been abandoned by some biographers and publishers. The pendulum has swung so far toward invasive techniques, and a refusal to afford any redress that both publishers and universities who lend credit by the use of their names should work to establish a code of fair dealing. This would include establishing a convention whereby those who have provided information and approve its use in the book are listed separately in the acknowledgements from those who do not. This, of course, would entail their being shown, before publication, the part which concerns them or uses their material. (A recent biographer was heard to complain that he could not be expected to check back with any of his informants as this might have meant his writing seventy letters. Lucky him, to have used so many helpful people, some of whom were then shocked and distressed by his book.) Ideally, informants should hold copyright in their testimony, thus guarding against its misuse and giving them the choice of making it available to other scholars.

The source of each observation should be listed by line number as well as page, leaving the reader in no doubt as to who said what. Informants should always be immediately given a copy of any tape recording of their meeting, so that they can clarify, check, or amplify for greater accuracy, after what is frequently only a single, informal interview. An example of impeccable method was that of Bernard Crick, who interviewed my husband and me, showing every mention of us in correspondence to or from Orwell, and inviting our memories, comments and corrections of fact.

But prior to these matters come the ethics of the decision to produce a biography at all. There is a strong case for subjects to have the legal right over permission for the publication of a biography of himself or herself in their lifetimes (issues of national and public interest make this problematical but not insoluble). In the absence of such a law, the would-be biographer and publisher have a moral responsibility to inform and consult a subject, and respect his or her wishes before the decision to commission the book is taken. After his or her death, the welfare of vulnerable survivors is to be considered, as it has been hitherto by responsible literary executors. But a spate of biographies is now in the offing which were undertaken in defiance of the wishes of subjects, their families or literary executors, yet none of the other people approached for information were informed of this fact. Letters requesting the help of friends and acquaintances, who have a right not to be misled, should make it clear if the book is unauthorized, and whether it is approved by the family. One must face the fact that to decline to see an unauthorized biographer, in loyalty to executors' wishes, may not contribute to the accuracy of that particular book. To do so because of doubts of the biographer's grasp of the background may serve to alter his views, or selection of evidence. The unauthorized author's public declarations of admiration for his subject's work, such as Hugh David's in the *Evening Standard*, 30 June 1992 – 'I'm a great Spender fan' – and his denials of prurient interest in the life of Stephen Spender, are scarcely borne out in the resulting book. A proportion of its numerous and fundamental errors of fact,[1] many total fictions, would be apparent to those who check David's sources against works by Isherwood and Spender,[2] a task the general reader is unlikely to undertake.

Even authorized biography presents its moral dilemmas, and often writers are subsequently troubled by the consequences in human terms of the choices they have made. Although the protagonists were no longer living, Richard Ellmann regretted having published very private letters of James Joyce. But it is to the living that serious, incalculable injury, even in health, can result. J.R. Ackerley wrote, concerning E.M. Forster 'I do think that it would be unconscionable of me to allow my letters, which give a unique and progressive account of Morgan's deeply felt emotional affairs with people still living, and still his close and constant friends, as well as my own, to be open to public inspection while they live.'[3] Our reputable biographers are sensitive to these issues, perhaps because they have gone deeper into the lives, of both principal and minor figures, they wish to understand. Unfortunately, the 'unconscionable' are all too often to be numbered among the 'unauthorized.'

13

Mather, Poe, Houdini

KENNETH SILVERMAN

If asked how I came to choose such worlds-apart subjects as Cotton Mather, Edgar Allan Poe, and Harry Houdini, I duck the question.* In reality the choice was over-determined – *way* over-determined – involving more attractions and repulsions, considerations pragmatic and ideal, than I would care to admit or anyone else to hear. The short answer is that all three men were Americans and traffickers in the supernatural – states of being that interest me. And some things that happened to them happened to me too; their lives suited what I felt equipped to say. You choose subjects the way Hemingway's bullfighters size up bulls, judging whether how they hook matches how you hold your cape. Some will show off your talents, others will probably kill you.

However like or unlike their subjects, the three books share the same assumptions about biography. Pressed for a working definition, I would say a biography is *the narrative dramatization of credible evidence about another person's life*. It aims not just at conveying information about the subject but more important at getting the reader to feel something about him. Like other genres, biography is a means of rousing pity, terror, and laughter – an axe, to use Kafka's image, for breaking the frozen sea that is the reader's heart.

NARRATIVE

The embattled lives of my minister, writer and magician lent themselves to storytelling. Mather, hobbled from childhood by a famous

---

*Kenneth Silverman, *The Life and Times of Cotton Mather* (1984), *Edgar A. Poe: Mournful and Never-ending Remembrance* (1992) and *Houdini!!!* (forthcoming). The protagonists in what follows are the generic Biographer, Subject, and Reader. To avoid nightmare-class pronoun problems, I treat them all as masculine. But my 'him' in these cases always means, inclusively, 'him or her'.

father and a career-threatening stammer, fought off an invasion of devils, an odious civic government, an epidemic of smallpox, spurned love, threats of debtors' prison, and the deaths of thirteen of his children. Poe wrestled orphanhood, a miserly guardian, failure at the University of Virginia, and expulsion from West Point, before losing to alcoholism, panic attacks, and hallucinations. Houdini daily escaped some new jam – handcuffs, straitjackets, roped packing-cases, riveted steamboilers, coffins nailed, screwed, buried in sand, sunk in water. The life of each man fit the classic prescription for a short-story: get someone in trouble and keep him there.

To say this another way, biographies are no disputations among the doctors. The narrative shouldn't be interrupted to explain how miserably some previous biographer erred. It takes all the canniness and patience you can muster to keep the subject and his world before the reader. Intruding the mere name of some biographer, and an echo of his style, jolts the reader out of the subject's timeframe, particularity, and world of discourse. And where the biographer fights a running battle with authorities the result isn't a biography at all but a biographical essay, a work of exposition more akin to history and criticism than to true biography. Debate belongs in the endnotes, in the reader's reach but out of the way of the story.

The same goes for secondary sources. Social and historical detail belongs in the narrative digested as scene-setting or envelope, the sources staying hidden in the notes. Clunky formulas of acknowledgement – 'As Jacques Authority has pointed out' – fill the reader's head with names he has no way of knowing he doesn't need to know. To read as narrative the text should look like narrative language, too; its appearance on the page shouldn't be flyspecked with superscript numbers. In their endnotes many biographers now identify sources by using key words from the text that connect them to the information they supply. Numeric dates can also command undue attention by their alien look, and usually have no narrative value: best to include none but essential dates. Time-spans can be printed as running section- and chapter-heads – 'June 1843–August 1844' – so that to orient himself the reader has only to glance at the top of the page.

Easy so far. But literary biography thwarts narration in posing its distinctive question: how are these particular works the products of this particular person? To demonstrate the link the biographer draws on literary criticism and, often, psychoanalytic ideas. Both stop narrative dead. The problems multiply with a writer of short works like Poe, who published a few dozen poems, about seventy tales, and hundreds of essays and reviews. Where such works appear regularly throughout a career, the narrative stands in danger of constant fragmentation. One of the Ten Commandments of literary biography may be, Thou shalt not choose a short-story writer (or 1775-poem Dickinson). With writers the stature of Mann, the works to be discussed can be not only so many but also so complex that interpretation displaces the narrative by overwhelming it.

There are some partial solutions. To avoid fragmentation, short works can be treated not serially but as a group upon their appearance in collected editions. The amount of expository deadwood can be reduced by moving plot-summaries, précis, and the like into appendices. The narrative itself sometimes presents chances to introduce critical analysis without greatly relaxing dramatic tension. Where the work is brief and closely connected to events, it can be discussed chronologically in place, in a quasi-narrative way. Poe happened to write 'The Poetic Principle,' for instance, while courting the well-off Rhode Island poet Sarah Helen Whitman. The important essay demanded discussion, yet that meant rupturing a thirty-page narrative of the main romantic affair in his life. I took advantage of the fact that he gave 'The Poetic Principle' as a lecture, with Whitman seated before him in the audience. In a few hybrid paragraphs that mix exposition and narration I tried to present the essay as at once something Poe wrote and something he did. Similarly I handled his megalomaniac cosmological treatise, *Eureka*, continuously with his madcap simultaneous courtship of four women and his suicide attempt, as one more expression of his emotional unravelling.

The works are smuggled into the flow of the writer's life by making exposition simulate narrative. This doesn't rule out treating them from non-biographical perspectives. It's a question of judging how much more critical comment can be added without leading the reader too far from the story. The principle is, Go as far out on the branch as you can without breaking the limb.

Contrarily, exegesis can be fenced off from narration. While moving the story ahead chronologically, the biographer passes by and saves up works for discussion until after some climax – a family death, move to a new city – someplace where the reader might like a breather before settling into some new phase of the action. In this catch-up section, literary interpretation can be introduced with a simple transition: 'Before leaving Richmond, Poe had managed to publish a half-dozen new tales,' etc. These readymade breaks seem natural places to cover other expository topics as well – history of ideas, social change, overarching developments.

Unfortunately the catch-up sections create their own problems. Chronology gets muddled. The biographer may be faced with a dozen unlike works written at different times calling for examination all at once. The reader's memory being short-lived, minor characters and budding events introduced before the interpretive break may have to be re-introduced after it. *Sauve qui peut.*

The technique of isolating exposition from narration works less troublesomely with psychoanalytic interpretation. Three papers on childhood mourning by the psychoanalyst Martha Wolfenstein, crystallized my thinking about Poe, whose mother died when he was about three.[1] Unable to conceive or accept the loss of a parent, Wolfenstein says, many children go on believing-and-not-believing that the parent still survives. (A remark by Poe, reported by a Philadelphia publisher, nicely illustrates such thinking: 'I believe that demons take advantage of the night to mislead the unwary' – 'although, you know,' he added, 'I don't believe in them.'[2]) Wolfenstein shows that the conflict not only persists in later life but also produces many derivatives. That pointed me to the yes-and-no quality of Poe's whole fictional world, where things are not only dead-and-alive but also both young and old, near and far, mechanical and organic.

But how to bring all this up without paralysing the action? Given its oddity and pervasiveness, Poe's oxymoronic thinking seemed to require a full explanation of the psychoanalytic theory that roots it in early loss. The cure, or at least remedy, was to emphasize the break. About seventy pages into the biography I sectioned off ten pages by a subhead: 'Remarks on Childhood Mourning.' In this emphatically marked compartment I treated the theory of pathological mourning once-for-all in expository language, alluding to it once or twice later on. What mattered, I thought, was to isolate the exposition from the story of Poe's life, letting echoes of it in the action ahead wink and wince at the reader as they would. In trying to minimize the drain on narrative energy and tension, the idea is to do it cleanly once and be done with it.

DRAMATIZATION

The nothing-but-narrative ideal doesn't aim at producing thrillers, although a great biography might read no less swiftly. Intensity of interest comes not simply from events, the lives of literary folk especially being notoriously devoid of incident but full of sitting. It comes from the subject's awareness of events, what Henry James called 'the *quality* of bewilderment characteristic of one's creature.' The most far-reaching comment about biography that I know appears in James's preface to *The Princess Casamassima*: 'the figures in any picture,' he says, 'the agents in any drama, are interesting only in proportion as they feel their respective situations.'[3] To count to the reader, events must count to the subject. Biography deals not so much with the trouble the subject has had as with the trouble he's seen.

Setting up shop inside his creature, where experience registers as pleasure, pain, or confusion, the biographer tries to keep consciousness present during narration. This means accenting not what happened to the subject but what it meant to him: not 'Mather's blissful marriage turned riotous,' but 'Mather looked on helplessly as his blissful marriage turned riotous.' Of course the determination to stress the subject's reactions requires his cooperation. He must have left behind extensive diaries, correspondence, and similar personal records. If not, he has to be dealt with mostly from outside (like Poe, alas), and is a dangerous bull. Other things being equal, good diary-keepers make good subjects. Autobiographical accounts are an exception, being usually more trouble than they're worth. Their (great) value lies in showing how the subject, at a certain time in his life, felt about himself. But many biographers mine them for details of his early years, about which they are often the only sources extant.

Used in this way, autobiographies are double trouble. As everyone knows, they can't be trusted. In several autobiographical sketches, Houdini states that he was born in Appleton, Wisconsin, on 6 April 1874; actually he was born in Budapest, Hungary, on 24 March. Even when autobiographical information is judged dependable, its use at the beginning of a biography contains a trap. In fairness to the reader, the biographer should suggest in the text the source of possibly-inexact or controversial information, a principle that obliges him to note that what he says about the subject's early life comes from the subject in old or middle age: 'In his later *Autobiography*, Franklin recorded that his mother. . . .' The biographer thus begins by assuming the very thing he means to demonstrate, the fully-imagined Franklin he has yet to create. In doing so, he refers the reader back to the established image of his subject, reinforcing the preconception he hopes to undo.

Autobiographies should be treated where the narrative comes to the time when they were written. They represent the subject's attempt at that moment to explain how he came to be what he is. An exception is when the biographer for some reason wants to open the life on a note of remembrance. Otherwise it's worth going to hell and back to avoid using later autobiographical material early-on, when it must be offered as fact rather than personal mythology.

Dramatizing a life involves recreating much more than what the subject did and felt. Like the neoclassic history-painter described by the eighteenth-century theorist Jonathan Richardson, the biographer must know 'the forms of the arms, the habits, customs, buildings, &c. of the age, and country, in which the thing was transacted.'[4] The subject's home and the scene of important events should be rendered from his own descriptions and from paintings, photographs, contemporary accounts, on-site visits. Hoping to depict Houdini's major feats as lived experience, not distant report, I wanted the reader to see the vaudeville houses and music halls in which he escaped from steamboilers and coffins, and the small industrial cities that made up his circuit, at the time he played them – Manchester in 1900, or Essen in 1912. The vital importance of even a few sentences of scene-setting made it worth running down playbills of the period, visiting what theatres survived, and collecting a shelf of Baedekers, 1910–15, describing Great Britain and Germany year by year.

The subject's appearance should also be made sensible, down to posture, mannerisms, quirks of dress. The descriptions can be reinvoked at high moments of the action to again conjure him up bodily. Secondary characters should be brought no less physically alive. In some biographies, the subject's friends and acquaintances exist as names instead of presences. But to serve dramatically, the attendants too need dirty fingernails, whispery voices, and bulging pockets, individualizing features that hard digging usually turns up.

By craft or instinct, many biographers use these dramatic techniques, mostly derived from nineteenth-century literary realism. Fewer have drawn on the aesthetic, Flaubertian branch of realism. In trying to hold the reader, the biographer can vary the prose surface from section to section, injecting fresh energy; syntax and sentence rhythm can be used as leitmotifs to signal the return of a character or theme; sound effects can enact important events by other means. Three months before Mather's death, New England was hit by the largest earthquake in its history. Luckily for a biographer, portentous after-shocks continued as he lay dying. To keep the fissuring and rumbling present, I loaded the narrative of his last days, maybe too insistently, with words like clatter, cracked, booming, bottom, bounded, Boston, and so on. The biographer can also forge symbols that alchemise the many elements of the life into one radiant image for the reader to take mentally home and retain. In the last words of his biography of Walt Whitman, Justin Kaplan memorably transmuted the poet's robust youth, lonely old age, and much more, into a symbolic ship at anchor.

CREDIBLE EVIDENCE

For all his freedom in using fictional devices, the biographer writes under rigid constraint, like someone composing a villanelle or fugue. He may never violate his evidence. It is all he has. The biography is not really a narrative of the life but of the available documents. Because the subject survives only in and through his and his contemporaries' letters, diaries, writings, photographs, you must find all of them you can. (I'm leaving aside interviews, having in mind subjects who died longer ago than living memory.) The ideal biographer may be a victim of the primal scene, someone obsessed with knowing secrets. For whatever reason he must have the joy of the hunt and keep his bags packed. The late editor of Mather's *Magnalia Christi Americana*, Kenneth Murdock, is said to have flown to South America for a footnote.

Where to start? The answer changes daily as electronic networks bring to life the researcher's dream of tapping all information on the planet by modem.[5] Meanwhile, for American writers – the subjects I know best – you start by locating the main repositories in the *National Union Catalogue of Manuscripts* and *American Literary Manuscripts*. You also send boilerplate inquiries to the likely places listed in the *AASLH Directory of Historical Societies*; search the AMC (archives/manuscripts) files of the RLIN online catalog; check the manuscript sales annually reported in *American Book Prices Current*; get yourself on the mailing lists of autograph dealers; advertise for material in collectors' journals and in literary papers like the *Times Literary Supplement*. I don't know why, but many biographers neglect census surveys, passport applications, real estate transactions, lawsuits, probate papers and the like, although public records preserve rich and unique evidence. Beyond this, you learn where things are by trying to get around. Way leads onto way, ever revealing new possible sources worth a visit, chat, call, letter.

When to stop? When you drop. You never find as much as there is; looking wider, deeper, longer always brings more. The rule applies even to carefully-catalogued collections and the best-trained archivists, who can't be expected to anticipate or grasp the subtleties of what qualifies as biographical material for you. The Library of Congress manuscript division, for example, houses the business records of Ellis and Allan, a Richmond firm co-owned by Poe's guardian, John Allan. They're their own library – 634 folios stuffed with inlaid correspondence, receipts, bills of lading. The Library photographed items that mentioned young Edgar Poe, and published them as a single reel of microfilm, 'Edgar Allan Poe Material, 1810–35.'

Handy as the film was, I re-sifted some 150 fat volumes of the manuscript hoard, covering the time until John Allan's death. The compiler(s), seeking mentions of Poe, had passed over scores of items about Allan and his wife: news of repeated rest-cures to restore broken health; lavish purchases of clothing, furniture, and liquor; a bankrupting business failure; flashes of jealousy, resentment, coldness. These looked like 'Edgar Allan Poe Material' to me. In fact the new information I gathered formed a detailed and wholly unfamiliar picture of Poe's homelife during childhood. The re-research even turned up mentions of Poe himself that had been overlooked.

In being presented to the reader, the documentary evidence should not stay inert. Many biographies follow the old Life-and-Letters model in reproducing without comment half-page chunks of correspondence or diaries, as if they had their own integrity and spoke for themselves. On the contrary, each scrap is wildly polysemous. A few lines in a letter often throw off facts and hints in every direction – about the subject's style of dress, habits of thought, occupation that day, relation to another person. Each bit should be separately kept for use. *Distribute*, although that means manufacturing a dozen notecards on the same few lines. My chopped-up sources go into parallel 4 × 6 files, one chronological, the other topical ('Appearance,' 'House,' 'Manchester'); many entries being only words-long, the files can bulge to 7500 cards.

As products of sorted and regrouped information-bytes, some narrative or descriptive statements come to be constituted from a half-dozen different sources. A one-sentence description of Poe's famous cottage at Fordham may merge a comment by him about the number of rooms, a visitor's remark about the size of the kitchen, a real-estate record giving the location, a photograph showing the garden. A good biographical sentence needs four endnotes to document; a great one needs five or six. The number measures the writer's attention to detail and dedication to dramatizing the past by reassembling its scattered record. The mosaic sentences mustn't show their seams, either. In aesthetic judgments of biographical writing, one essential standard is this dense, intricate blending of source material.

Zealous empiricism of course doesn't guarantee truth. The documents can be wrong – newspapers especially – and subjects can lie. Houdini gave hundreds of interviews to reporters as eager for good copy as he was to grab headlines; almost nothing he said to the press or is supposed to have said can be believed. The biographer of the famous long-dead also has to weed out florid overgrowths of gossip. Stories have come down from the nineteenth century that as a teenager Poe ran away to Russia and that in adulthood he rogered his mother-in-law. Every literary hanger-on of the time heard him recite 'The Raven' and saw him drunk: everyone wants a piece of the cross. Ideally the biographer requires two eyewitness accounts of every important episode; at the least he looks for corroboration.

The record is not only shaky but also full of holes. For one twenty-nine-month stretch, Poe's life is nearly a complete blank. In like circumstances, some biographers speculate on what the subject 'may' or 'must' have done, thought, or felt. But speculation is meaningless, because ignorance gives it no ground. If you can conjecture one state of affairs you can conjecture any. Poe may have been in debt and drinking heavily during the missing years, as at other times; then again he may have peddled graham crackers, mended bagpipes, or gone to clown school. You have to interpret the evidence, but can't divine it.

For the sake of coherence, the temptation is to pretend the gaps don't exist. Dwight Macdonald advised a young biographer: 'you're the boss, not the Facts. . . . Be a literary man and not a research mouse . . . simplify and generalize.'[6] But if the biographer means to grant the subject its own life and respect its otherness, the facts do the bossing. When important information is missing, the reader should be told, awkward as that may be. Squeaky-clean continuity represents a false claim of completeness. In this respect, biographies shouldn't read too well.

ANOTHER PERSON'S LIFE

Biography is a peculiar genre, journalistic in content, classical in form. Because each new age wants to know different things about historic figures, their stories must constantly be told anew, so that even well-made biographies have shelf-lives of only a generation or two. The few that survive do so as literature, that is by virtue of their style. At the same time the shape of biography changes little. It remains linear because inherently bound to the cycle of life and death, to a subject that unhappily has built-in closure.

Formal breakthroughs are possible and would be welcome. But don't expect them from attempts to deflect attention from the subject toward the method, the biographer, or the context. Some academic theorists call for 'problematizing' the form – to use their Eisenhowerism – 'foregrounding' the biographer and the labyrinth of textual truth. A few lively biographies have been written in a self-reflexive spirit, such as Julian Barnes's *Flaubert's Parrot*. But how many would one care to read that drew from every life the same lesson of indeterminacy? And to date, most biographers who have spotlighted themselves have exposed someone with little personality and nothing to say. Don't bank, either, on academic ideologues who propose 'contextualizing' the subject, as if his difficult life had been merely illustrative, and counted most by serving them to demonstrate commodity-fetishism.

The biographer lives with the queasy knowledge that another person's life must remain in essence unknowable and unrevealed. He creates at best a simile, a resemblance, a composite police sketch based on fleeting observation. Nevertheless the likeness always tells us something, not everything but something, about the subject, something moreover real and dependable. The challenge is to stay true to the facts but move the reader by the spectacle of another soul's journey through time.

14

Breaking In

ANDREW MOTION

In September 1946, when he was twenty-four, Philip Larkin went to work as sub-librarian at University College, Leicester. Within three weeks he had met Monica Jones, a lecturer in the English Department. After three years they had become lovers. After another six months Larkin left Leicester for the library at Queen's University, Belfast, where he stayed for five years, seeing Monica regularly but at widely-spaced intervals. In 1955 he was appointed Librarian at the University of Hull, and remained there for the last thirty years of his life. During this time he and Monica took annual holidays together, met at least once a month, wrote to each other and/or spoke on the telephone nearly every day. The relationship was in certain respects deeply troubled (by jealousies, by distance), and in others very happy. Monica was Larkin's steadfast companion and his soul-mate. He dedicated *The Less Deceived* to her: it was the only collection of poems he dedicated to anyone.

In September 1961 Monica bought a small house in Haydon Bridge in Northumberland, on the main Newcastle–Carlisle road. (Her family had originally come from that part of the world.) She meant it to be a bolt-hole – somewhere she might escape the various worries of her private life and her university work. Larkin was initially suspicious of the house but soon admiring. He took holidays there, hunkered down in it for weekends, always visited at New Year. When he wouldn't or couldn't leave Hull, Monica was often in Haydon Bridge alone – writing Larkin letters, waiting for him to ring. The house was their special place, their burrow.

In June 1983, when she was sixty-one, recently retired from Leicester, and living in Haydon Bridge more or less full-time, Monica developed shingles. Larkin, who was staying, took charge. He ferried her south to Hull and put her in hospital, where she lay half-blinded and in great pain for several days. Then he brought her back to his own house in Hull. She stayed ten months – until the following April – before returning to Haydon Bridge, meaning to re-start her independent life. But she was still unwell, and anyway Larkin missed her. Within a few days he had decided to collect her again. He helped her pack, then sat in the car while she checked for last things, drew the curtains, switched off the electricity at the meter, and locked the front door. Anxiously, he drove her back to Hull.

Larkin thought Monica was fatally ill. In fact, he was. Within a year he was in hospital for tests: on 2 December 1985 he died of cancer. Monica stayed in Hull – depressed, sick and exhausted. She wanted her own life back but couldn't reach it. She worried about her house in Haydon Bridge but was too ill to get herself there.

Early in 1986 Monica asked me to write Larkin's biography, and over the next few years we saw a great deal of each other. She sat in what had once been Larkin's chair, his tweed coat still slung over the arm. I sat on the sofa, his Rowlandson watercolor on the dark green wall behind me. Sometimes I formally interviewed her; sometimes we just chatted. Sometimes we looked at photographs of him or by him; sometimes we read his books. There was no hurry. She had known Larkin better than anyone. I had to ransack her memory.

Monica said nothing about the letters Larkin had written her. If I asked where they were she would shrug – lighting another cigarette, pouring another drink. Did this mean she didn't want me to see them? Or had they, like his diaries, been destroyed? She wasn't telling.

One day out of the blue she said most of the letters were in Haydon Bridge. Why didn't we drive up together to get them? It was a forlorn hope – she was too ill – yet she didn't want me to go without her. The house was theirs: a secret place, where she and Larkin had lived to the exclusion of all others. Dark-curtained and unvisited, it held their continuing, unbroken life together. Once the door had been opened, that life would be over.

Months passed. Monica grew more frail. Eventually she decided I would have to go alone. I drove up with a friend from Hull, Marion Shaw, in the autumn of 1989. As far as I knew, no one had been into the house for five years.

We roller-coasted the wet road towards Hexham, then on. Rain was swirling in from the North Sea behind us. So much had fallen in recent weeks, the moors were yellow and sour-looking. As we ducked down into Haydon Bridge, streams bulged in the ditches beside us.

The house was even smaller than I'd expected, and uglier. Packed into a tight row near the Old Bridge, on the main road, it had a jaded white front, a slate roof, plain modern windows and a front door which opened straight off the street. I got the key from a neighbor and opened up – but the door was stuck. Peering through the letter-box, the rain falling on my neck and back, I could see why. There was a mound of junk mail on the mat: offers of free film, estate agents' bumf, cards from taxi companies and window cleaners.

I shoved the door violently and we were in. A tiny box of a hall; the sitting-room to the left; stairs rising straight ahead. The stairs looked crazy. There was no carpet (just the pale section where a carpet had once been) and at the sides of each step – cans of food. One of these had leaked, oozing blood-colored treacle into a puddle at my feet. I tried to wipe it up, scrape it up, somehow get rid of it, with a piece of junk mail. It was impossible. In the end I hid it beneath a few bright envelopes.

The smell was worse when I turned on the electricity. Sweet open-air dampness like a rotten log – but also fusty. And there was noise too, noise I couldn't recognize. A roaring, but somehow subdued. When I turned into the sitting-room I understood. Outside the window at the back, beyond a cramped cement yard and a tow-path, there flowed a gigantic river. The Tyne; invisible from the road. Within the first few seconds of looking, I saw a full-grown tree sweep past, then heard the trunk grinding against the bridge away to my left, out of sight.

The window was broken – a hole like a star-burst and slivers of glass on the purple carpet.

We weren't the first people here for years, we were the second and third – at least the second and third. The drawers in a sideboard lolled open, empty; in the grate, jagged pieces of crockery poked out of a sootfall; there was a dark circle in the dust on a table where a vase had stood. And there were books all over the floor – books flung about for the hell of it – and a deep scar on the window-seat where something heavy had been manhandled into the yard then away along the towpath.

We tiptoed through the shambles, closing up, straightening, tidying, our hands immediately grey with dust. It was wet dust, sticking to us and clinging in our noses and lungs. Monica hadn't told me where I might find the letters, but it didn't matter. They were every-where. In books, down the side of a chair, under a rug, on the window-seat. A few lay flat and saturated in the yard, scrabbled out when the last burglar left.

It was the same upstairs, though the dust seemed lighter there, maybe because the rain had eased off outside and the sun was starting to break through. The river sounded quieter, too, and I could see a family on the opposite bank – a man, a woman and two children, walking a dog.

I went into the lumber room, into a jungle of clothes and hangers which had a small box at its heart, stuffed with letters.

Nothing in the bathroom.

In the smaller bedroom: under the window overlooking the river, a bed with letters both inside and underneath it, and a cupboard crowded with damp dresses which tore when I touched them.

In the larger bedroom: more letters in books, an empty case of wine, an ironing board with a half-ironed dress draped across it.

When I got downstairs I realized I was breathing in gulps, as if I were swimming.

We counted the letters into plastic bags. There were nearly two hundred of them. Then we went through the house again, found the last handful, turned off the electricity, locked up, returned the key to the neighbor, arranged for the window to be repaired and climbed into the car. The sun had gone in; it was starting to rain again. Larkin had sat in the same place, squinting at the little house, feeling anxious. I felt exhilarated and ashamed.

I wasn't the last. A week or so after I'd taken the letters back to Monica, a van drew up outside the house in Haydon Bridge and two people got out, kicked open the front door and stole nearly everything inside. If the letters had still been there, they would have gone too. By the time this happened, I'd read them – and two hundred or so more, that Monica revealed Larkin had written to her in Leicester.

15

Shilling Lives: An Interview

ANTHONY CURTIS

INTERVIEWER: Anthony Curtis you were the literary editor of two British national newspapers, *The Sunday Telegraph* and *The Financial Times*, over three decades, that is, from 1960 to 1990. . . .

CURTIS: Guilty.

INTERVIEWER: During that period you must have had dozens of biographies pass through your hands and among them some that have made a great contribution to the genre.

CURTIS: It was difficult to keep track of all the biographies sent in for review. I frequently wished I had double the space at my disposal in order to cover them adequately.

INTERVIEWER: Were biographies the most numerous of all the kinds of book submitted?

CURTIS: There were never as many biographies and autobiographies as there was fiction. About half the books sent in for review were fiction. That will always be the largest category on the shelves in any newspaper lit. ed.'s office.

INTERVIEWER: Yet looking through some of your pages, and at some of those edited by your successors, and in other newspapers, the main review, the one leading the page, often seems to be of a new biography.

CURTIS: You are absolutely right. Write a biography and you get scores of lead reviews everywhere; write a novel and unless you happen to be William Golding or Truman Capote, or someone of that celebrity, half the papers ignore your book altogether. That's the novelist's grievance; until, that is, he or she writes a biography.

I once went to a Society of Bookmen dinner in London at which the guest of honor was J.B. Priestley. 'If there are any literary editors present,' he growled, 'I do wish they would abandon the insulting way that new novels are at present reviewed, in ill-assorted batches of four or five at a time, and give them the same kind of treatment they give to biographies.' According to Priestley, writing a biography was a soft option; all the writer had to do was to go to a library and look up a few facts. 'Money for old rope' he called it.

INTERVIEWER: Try telling that to Michael Holroyd or the late Richard Ellmann.

CURTIS: Quite.

INTERVIEWER: But why do books pages so often lead with the review of a biography?

CURTIS: Biography is the lit. ed.'s best friend because it is reckoned to contain that mysterious entity 'news value.' Even the biography of a minor statesman, politician or literary figure arouses expectations of an interesting, lively read that the appearance of a new novel does not.

INTERVIEWER: (dubiously) Does a biography always have such an inbuilt advantage over a novel in getting reviewed?

CURTIS: Almost always. Unless the subject of the biography is totally obscure the reader has his curiosity aroused before he starts reading the review. He and the reviewer share some common ground at the outset. In a fiction or a poetry review, the reviewer has to define or somehow create that common ground. It is rather different around Booker Prize time in October and November; then the fiction reviews do arouse keen interest among people who do not normally read them. That is one of the beneficial effects of the prize.

INTERVIEWER: What you seem to be saying is that with a biography, the reviewer reviews the subject – the man or woman – rather than the book or the author?

CURTIS: If the reviewer is any good he or she does both. If he has interesting views of his own about the subject of the biography let us hear them by all means but not – I repeat, not – at the expense of the book. In the old days the leading Sunday book-reviewers, people like Edmund Gosse, Desmond MacCarthy, Harold Nicolson would aim in their weekly reviews at giving a pen-portrait of the subject; much of it was, I agree, their own views, and then somewhere along the line they would introduce their comments on the book. But that style of literary journalism has gone right out of fashion.

INTERVIEWER: They probably knew as much about the subject as the author of the book.

CURTIS: Certainly they tried awfully hard to give that impression.

INTERVIEWER: Need the reviewer always be an authority on the subject?

CURTIS: That raises the question of who is qualified to review any particular biography. It is one to which every lit. ed. has to give careful thought each time he sends out a biography. Clearly complete ignorance of the subject or only the sketchiest knowledge is not a good qualification in a reviewer however bright. But there are some reviewers, people whose main activity is reviewing, who educate themselves as they go along. Such a reviewer probably starts with only a modicum of knowledge but is prepared to read all the previous biographies as well as the one under review. V.S. Pritchett, for example, built up his amazing erudition in that way. You may get an excellent review from this type of reviewer, one that is more just and more 'accessible' to the ordinary reader than a review written by an acknowledged authority. A lit. ed. needs to be wary about giving the book for review to the author of another biography on the same subject (either one that has already appeared or is about to appear). It is almost impossible to be fair to a rival book, either you bend over too far in its favor to prove your integrity or you let professional pique drive you into writing a hatchet-job.

INTERVIEWER: Can we confine ourselves for the rest of this interview to literary biography, the biographies of writers? It seems to be swamping the market at present.

CURTIS: It has been for many years past. When I ceased to be literary editor and became solely a reviewer, in my first two years the biographies I reviewed included *Young Betjeman* by Bevis Hillier, *Eddy: The Life of Edward Sackville-West* by Michael De-la Noy, *William Plomer* by Peter F. Alexander, *Ackerley: A Life of J.R. Ackerley* by Peter Parker, *C.S. Lewis* by A.N. Wilson, *William Gerhardie* by Dido Davies, *A.A. Milne* by Ann Thwaite, *Paul Scott* by Hilary Spurling, *Constance Garnett: A Heroic Life* by Richard Garnett, *Gerard Manley Hopkins* by Robert Bernard Martin. . . .

INTERVIEWER: You have made your point. But do all these biographies really find readers and justify themselves in commercial terms? What are the economics of it?

CURTIS: (*laughing*) You should ask a publisher that question, someone who commissions these biographies and pays the author of them an advance against royalties while they are being written, or an agent, someone like Christopher Sinclair-Stevenson, Ion Trewin, Richard Cohen. But – to give a short answer – my impression is that, yes, most of them do find a sufficient quantity of readers to justify them otherwise they would not get published. There are instances of excessively high advances being paid to some outstanding biographers of the great modern authors whose agents have jacked the ante up into the stratosphere; but nonetheless it clearly is a booming literary industry. Readers, purchasers of books and library-borrowers, appear to be completely hooked on the lives of writers. They do not seem to be able to get enough of them.

INTERVIEWER: Why is that? Many writers lead very dull lives, don't they? What is so thrilling about someone sitting at a desk every day writing for long hours?

CURTIS: That writer-person must get his/her material from somewhere. Not all of it comes, as it were, from inside his own head. At some point he has engaged with the real world – in childhood, in youth, in middle-age, in old age – then he had an experience that eventually grew by means of the imaginative process into a work. The fascination of a biography of a writer, indeed of any kind of artist, lies in seeing where the work had its origin.

INTERVIEWER: Surely that is all secondary.

CURTIS: Sorry, but I'm not clear what you mean by 'secondary.'

INTERVIEWER: Secondary, to appreciating, enjoying, experiencing the work. The greater the work, the less it matters what the historical or personal event in the writer's own life that may have triggered it was. I don't give two hoots whether Shakespeare was gay or straight or both. Nor do I care whether he was an Anglican or a Catholic. At the end of the day all that matters to me is *Romeo and Juliet, Midsummer Night's Dream, Hamlet, King Lear* and the rest of the canon as we experience them in the theater or direct from the printed page.

CURTIS: That is the purist view. I respect it and I share it – at, as you say, the end of the day; but around the middle of the day I must confess to being deeply curious about the man who wrote those plays and wish I knew more about his life. I am grateful to a Shakespearean expert like Stanley Wells who in *Shakespeare: A Dramatic Life* sets out to authenticate all the biographical facts about him. Wells says we know everything concerning Shakespeare's life except what we should really like to know: such things as how he got from his boyhood in Stratford to his apprenticeship in London as an actor and a writer for the theatre. In that respect I even find myself being drawn down the more speculative biographical paths like those opened up by E. Honigmann who suggests that it might have been via the household of some great nobleman in the North of England where the young Shakespeare was employed.

INTERVIEWER: Yes, I too am curious to know more about his professional life but even if the speculations about crucial periods in it could be proved to be true without any shadow of doubt, would they in any way enhance one's understanding of *Hamlet*?

CURTIS: They might. They just might. They might help us to discover what Eliot thought was the 'objective correlative' that lies outside the play, some experience of evil to which the play was a reaction, and which is not apparent from the events it depicts.

But let's bring the discussion nearer home, to the twentieth century and the writers of the modern movement. Unlike Shakespeare they did draw directly on their own lives for their material and they made no secret of the fact. Surely in reading Lawrence's novels it is an advantage to know about his family, about the mining and farming areas at the end of the last century near where he lived and about the factory in which he worked where they made artificial limbs, all the things John Worthen tells us in his *D.H. Lawrence: The Early Years 1885–1912*. Or in reading Conrad to know about the training required for entry into the British Merchant Navy at the end of the nineteenth century, about the kind of contract that existed between the captain of a vessel and its owners, about the conditions when sail was being replaced by steam, all that Jeffrey Meyers goes into in his *Joseph Conrad*. It does help one's understanding of the novels and tales quite considerably, doesn't it?

INTERVIEWER: You could get all that from a good introduction just as easily.

CURTIS: But Worthen and Meyers go into much more than just that. Worthen goes into the question of women's education in late Victorian England. He even shows that Lawrence and Frieda never really eloped; they both just happened to be in Germany at the same time.

INTERVIEWER: (*drily*) How very convenient for them!

CURTIS: A biography is essentially a work of history, a unique kind of genre filtering history through the life of an outstanding individual, integrating the public archive with the private archive.

INTERVIEWER: But with a writer the main archive is the work. We wouldn't be interested in Conrad or even aware that he existed, if he had just stayed on in the Merchant Navy until retirement and then become a garrulous old salt haunting the bars of the yacht clubs. It is because he left the navy, learnt English under Garnett and wrote *Chance, Youth, Lord Jim, Nostromo* etc., that he became interesting. Similar with Lawrence, if he had remained a teacher we would not care tuppence about him. And I do not see that it makes a scrap of difference to either history or the work to know, as Meyers claims, that Conrad slept with an American journalist called Jean Anderson when she came to write an article about him.

CURTIS: Meyers suggests that she was the model for Rita de Lastaola in *The Arrow of Gold*.

INTERVIEWER: What a triumph! To have been the model for the heroine of Conrad's least read novel. Nor do I care much how many lovers Frieda had before and after she had Lawrence. Every biography nowadays has its quota of 'revelations.' In filtering what you call history the modern biographer often descends to the level of the writer of a gossip column.

CURTIS: Come, come! Be honest and stop sounding like Mrs Grundy. As human beings we are all fascinated to know that Conrad may have had a mistress and that Frieda betrayed Lawrence with someone called Harold Hobson (not the drama critic, another one). But what we have been seeing and are still witnessing in biography is an over-reaction against the reticence that used to be imposed on the writer of biography. You remember how Maugham satirized it in *Cakes and Ale* in relation to Hardy. Hardy even went to the length of writing his own official biography leaving out everything about himself he did not want made public. The book he wrote was published posthumously as if it had been written by Florence Hardy, his wife.

INTERVIEWER: Hardy was the soul of reticence. Not even Robert Gittings was able to penetrate all of the defences he erected. Well done, Hardy, I say!

CURTIS: What seems to me remarkable is how long that code of reticence lasted; it continued well into our own time. Harold Nicolson for instance practiced it. He was eminent as a diplomat, a literary critic and as a biographer. He once wrote an article on 'The Practice of Biography' in which he said: '. . . the necessity of maintaining a certain level of taste, consideration, caution, and kindliness will certainly prevent him [the biographer] from revealing the truth in its most naked form.'

INTERVIEWER: When did he say that?

CURTIS: When do you think?

INTERVIEWER: Some time in the 1930s at a guess.

CURTIS: No, it is from an article published originally in *The American Scholar* in 1954.

INTERVIEWER: Good heavens! It sounds light years away.

CURTIS: Yet it was formulated only thirteen years before Big Bang.

INTERVIEWER: What on earth was Big Bang?

CURTIS: Big Bang in this context was the appearance of the first edition of Michael Holroyd's biography of Lytton Strachey in 1967. It was then that the Age of Reticence was succeeded by the Age of Candor.

INTERVIEWER: Hadn't Strachey inaugurated the Age of Candor himself in 1916 in *Eminent Victorians*?

CURTIS: Ah yes! But that was loaded candor, not always completely accurate. It was the candor of the caricaturist applied to historical figures. It can be very penetrating and is still great fun to read.

INTERVIEWER: Candor, complete honesty in personal relations and critical responses, was the great Bloomsbury rallying cry. It has a lot to answer for.

CURTIS: They weren't quite so keen on it when it was applied to themselves in public. Originally Holroyd had to give some of the supporting cast fictitious names. People who were still alive when the book first came out and might have made a fuss. In the most recent edition – the revised one of 1994 – the footnotes by James Strachey have been scrapped and the fictitious names replaced by real ones. Complete candor now reigns.

INTERVIEWER: It reigns everywhere in biography from those of the royals downwards. In the post-Holroyd era readers of biographies of the recently dead are in danger of being deafened by the sound of skeletons falling out of cupboards.

CURTIS: The last decisive blow was struck by Nigel Nicolson when in 1973 he published *Portrait of A Marriage*. After that bombshell no biographical holds would be barred. It was the end of his father's Queensberry rules.

INTERVIEWER: At least that was a primary document. Without realizing it you've made the case for reading a major writer's letters and journals. Aren't they always so much more enlightening than a biography? I feel so much closer to Wilde when I read his letters edited by Rupert Hart-Davis than I do when I read any biographer, even one as good as Ellmann.

CURTIS: Why cannot you read both? Harold Nicolson's *Diaries* are essential reading but so is James Lees-Milne's biography of him in two volumes. Lees-Milne maintains Nicolson's own criterion of 'a certain level of taste, consideration, caution, and kindliness.' Another advantage is that Lees-Milne writes just as well as the man he is writing about. But on the other hand he does not lack candor. Nicolson's amours with other men are discussed and Lees-Milne concludes that Nicolson was someone who never really grew up. But it is also written out of a great admiration and affection for him.

INTERVIEWER: Lees-Milne must be unique. Does he deal with Vita too?

CURTIS: Yes, but through the eyes of Harold. If you want to see her life in full you will need to read the biography of Vita by Victoria Glendinning. Just as Holroyd sees Carrington only in relation to Lytton. If you want to find out about the rest of her life – her affair with Mark Gertler, for example – you'll need to read *Carrington: A Life of Dora Carrington* by Gretchen Gerzina, the edition of her letters and diaries edited by David Garnett and the parts of the diaries of Frances Partridge that mention her. Mrs Partridge is the last living link with all those people.

INTERVIEWER: It seems to be a wonderfully self-perpetuating industry.

CURTIS: There is usually a primary biography written by a relation or a close friend that is then complemented by subsequent ones written by a scholar and professional biographer. In some cases one is enough: after Richard Garnett's recent biography of his grandmother Constance I would not have thought another one would be required. Quentin Bell's life of his aunt must be the starting-point for any biographical understanding of Virginia Woolf. It has an authenticity that no subsequent one can ever match but it also has its limitations. The most recent one by James King, a Canadian professor of literature, takes in all that has been published since Bell and integrates the life with the work much more fully.

INTERVIEWER: Okay. Then let us have a statute of biographical limitation: just one primary biography and one good later one and call it a day.

CURTIS: People who write biographies for a living would hate to hear you say that. They reckon that there is always room for one more. Each biographer brings a fresh set of insights and attitudes to the subject. King (who previously did a good job on Herbert Read) is certainly not going to be the last biographical word on Mrs Woolf. But with many of the lesser figures one biography may be enough to satisfy all needs. I cannot see anyone else tackling Sacheverell Sitwell in a hurry after Sarah Bradford's go at him, or Edward Sackville-West after Michael De-la Noy's or Gerald Brennan after Jonathan Gathorne-Hardy's or Ottoline Morrell after Miranda Seymour's. But you never know.

16

The Authorized Biographer

ERIC JACOBS

The word 'unauthorized' on the cover of a biography raises gleeful expectations of gossip and scandal, at least of uncomfortable disclosures the biographer's subject would far prefer be kept hidden. The unauthorized biographer cuts a matchingly bold figure as a relentless seeker after truth, one who will not be silenced, a fearless fellow daring to go where no man or woman has gone before.

Alongside this hero, the authorized biographer seems a poor, crawly sort of creature. Since it is his subject who has authorized him, the subject must have complete control over what is published, turning the writer into a mere serf, a bought man, firmly wedged in the pocket of the person he is supposed to be telling us the whole truth about, so not to be trusted for one moment.

I noticed these assumptions in almost everyone I talked to during the two years or so I spent researching and writing the authorized biography of Kingsley Amis. 'What are you up to these days?' people would ask and when I told them they would exclaim in astonishment: 'But he's alive, isn't he?' 'Very much so,' I would reply, then watch their reaction, which became as predictable as the passage of a coin dropping from level to level through a slot machine. 'Amis is co-operating, so must have control – therefore the book will be the version of himself he wants the world to see and Jacobs has become his willing tool. Oh, well. Mustn't be too hard on the chap. He probably needs the money.' This chain of thought was no less clear for being usually left unspoken. Friends would pass briskly on to other matters, courtesy deterring them from pursuing further the doubts about me that were, from their faces, evidently multiplying in their minds.

I entirely understand these feelings and might well have shared them at the start if the authorized biographer in question had not been myself, to whom I naturally extended the benefit of all doubts. In these days when image counts for so much – to politicians, performers, artists, writers – trying to take control of it makes obvious sense. And what better way of doing that could there be than licensing some tame hack to turn out a charmingly sanitized picture of oneself for the public to admire?

But, having now actually written an authorized biography, I see things very differently. Whatever may be the case with others, my subject's co-operation proved no liability or limitation at all. Amis did not try to censor what I wrote, least of all anything that might seem to show him in an unfavorable light. When he read through my typescript he was more concerned with defects in my punctuation than faults in the image of him I had drawn.

In Amis's forbearance with his red censor's pencil I was un-doubtedly very lucky. One can easily think of potential subjects who would deploy a much heavier hand. But it was not just in this forbearance that I felt myself fortunate in working with Amis rather than without him. There are many reasons why, the first and most clearcut being the capacity contact gives to learn or check basic facts.

To take just one example from many, let me cite the question of how and when Amis met the woman who was to become his second wife, Elizabeth Jane Howard, like him a novelist. The answer is both wildly implausible – much too far-fetched to be used in a work of fiction – and wholly fitting. They met when Amis took part (along with Romain Gary, Carson McCullers and Joseph Heller) in a semi-nar on 'Sex in Literature' at the Cheltenham Literary Festival, of which Howard was that year's artistic director. I know this because Amis told me. But would I have been able to discover it for myself?

Clues were available. I already knew that Amis had been on the seminar panel from a newspaper cutting I had come across in the voluminous files on him kept at the library of the *Daily Mail* in London. I saw from those cuttings too that Howard was that year's festival director. Clearly, there was some significance to be worked up from these two facts, since less than a year after Cheltenham Amis and Howard were well known to be living together. But exactly what significance was far from clear. I can imagine myself embroidering some fanciful scenario in which Howard, having already met and fall-en distractedly in love with Amis, contrives to get him an invitation to her festival so that they can pursue their furtive affair behind the scenes. It would have been utter rubbish, but no piece of paper – diary, letter or what have you – has come my way that would either contradict such a speculation or confirm the fact that Cheltenham was indeed the fateful meeting-place from which wheels started rolling towards marriage. It needed Amis or Howard to point me to the facts.

But, you might ask, if a biographer has no access to his subject, might he not turn instead to people who know him: friends, lovers, relatives, colleagues? The biographer very well might. If he did, though, he would most likely discover they would tell him nothing without the approval of their friend or acquaintance, the biographer's subject. Later, I realized that I might have found out the significance of Cheltenham from Amis's first wife Hilly. But would she have told me about that or anything else if I did not have Amis's authority behind me? I doubt it. People are loyal to their friends, even to ex-husbands. The unauthorized biographer is all too likely to finish up talking to his subject's enemies alone, which is probably why such books so often reflect a mood of gratuitous and rancid hostility.

Armed with Amis's consent, I found many of his friends ready to help me as best they could. But I soon discovered problems with such sources, however helpful they meant to be. They were apt to think they knew more about Amis than they actually did. One of the things that most surprised me by the end of my inquiries was the realization of how little people really know about friends or even intimates. Perhaps it is a condition of friendship that one accepts friends for what they care to reveal about themselves and does not probe into their business like a nosey biographer. But that is a large question. Let me here just mention three examples of the fallibility of the best-intentioned informants.

The first example comes from Amis's schooldays. One fellow pupil of Amis's at the City of London School described to me in persuasive detail a plot to have him made a school prefect. When the existing prefects refused to elect him to join their number, a friend of Amis's who happened to be the school's head boy just added Amis's name to the list and thus created a fait accompli. This looked like a tasty little tale of teenage corruption to put some spice into the fairly thin brew of stories about Amis's schooldays I had accumulated. But alas, it wasn't true. The school rules made it difficult if not impossible and besides the head boy himself told me he had entered into no such conspiracy.

The second example involves a casual remark thrown out by one of Amis's Oxford friends, a man of impeccable reputation, a retired ambassador, who had no reason or incentive whatever to make things up. We were chatting about Amis in a rambling way when he suddenly threw out a stunning aside. 'Of course,' he said, 'you know that Kingsley won the M.C.' What! Amis had been awarded the Military Cross, Britain's second highest medal for soldierly valor, during his Army service in the Second World War! But Amis had always told me he had done his very best to keep out of the line of fire and from what I knew of him I believed him completely when he said it. And yet the ambassador was so sure he was right he had hardly thought it worth mentioning because I was bound to know about it already. Whether or not somebody has won a medal is one of those things it's easy to check and I soon found that Amis had done no such thing. The ambassador wasn't lying. He had just got it wrong, perhaps misreading M.A. as M.C. in some reference book.

My third example has to do with the goings-on in the somewhat unorthodox Amis household of the 1990s. Amis now shares a house in London with his first wife, Hilly, and her third husband, Lord Kilmarnock. A close friend and neighbor told me conversationally one day that Kilmarnock climbed the stairs from his basement flat regularly every morning to bring Amis a cup of tea in bed. That was just the nugget of information I was looking for, something that would sum up the state of affairs in the odd Amis household in one short but telling anecdote. But again, it wasn't true. And again Amis's friend wasn't lying to deceive me. He had simply got it wrong.

These little incidents taught me a sharp lesson, by the way. For they showed me how eager I was to be led by the nose into error. I was perfectly willing to embrace wholly new and unexpected versions of my subject, to rewrite my book on such themes as 'Amis, the schoolboy cheat,' or 'Amis, the unsung wartime hero,' or 'Amis, the tyrant in his own home.' I wanted these stories to be true so that they could liven up my book. As someone who had watched from the sidelines a decade earlier as the whole hierarchy of the London *Sunday Times*, from Rupert Murdoch on down, was sucked into believing in the fake Hitler Diaries because they wanted them to be authentic so that they could score a world-class journalistic coup, I should have known better.

Faulty memories also help to make the biographer's life difficult. People not only misunderstand, they misremember too. I can't resist describing a ripe example of both factors operating together to produce a rich pickle of confusions. Amis had told me a story about an encounter he had had with a member of the Royal family at a luncheon in a private house. So I wrote to the man who had been Amis's host to ask if he could confirm the story and add any details he might remember. The host wrote back promptly and courteously enough, but only to say that there was no truth in the story whatsoever. There couldn't be, he said. He had not entertained this particular member of the Royal family before the 1970s; Amis had died in 1969; therefore Amis could never have been at a luncheon with the aforementioned Royal personage. His seeming conviction that Amis had been dead for a quarter of a century did not prevent the host from inviting Amis to luncheon once more, a few months after his letter to me. Truly, the biographer's course is not a straight one.

It is not only sources close to a biography's subject that get muddied by defective memory. The subject's own memory is just as likely to get muddied as anybody else's. If you ask a man in 1993 what he was doing in 1946, he is apt to give you a sketchy answer. When I asked Amis, he could remember that he was back at Oxford from the war, working towards his exams, courting the girl who was to become his first wife – that sort of thing. The same minimal recollections were all he could tell me about many other years too. To put flesh on such bare bones, contemporary evidence is invaluable. Amis's letters, particularly to his friend Philip Larkin the poet, provided me with a lot of the flesh I needed. Conventional tools of research like these are vital to any biographer, authorized or otherwise, writing about someone still alive or dead ten or a hundred years.

(If I can indulge in a digression, I should like to spend one bracketed paragraph pursuing a personal vendetta against the Bodleian Library in Oxford for making it so difficult to get hold of Amis's letters to Larkin. The Bodleian first refused access on the grounds that it was library policy not to disclose the papers of living people, since what they had written might be hurtful to other people still alive. I pointed out that a writer's death offered no guarantee of protection to the living. Larkin himself was dead; his letters had been published; they were offensive to a number of people still alive, including Amis. So library policy was wholly ineffective in achieving the aim it set itself. But the Bodleian was unmoved, either by me or the Chancellor of Oxford, Lord Jenkins, or the then Secretary for Education, John Patten, who pitched in on my behalf. Then Amis himself had an idea. Why did he not write to the Bodleian and ask for copies of his own letters, the cost of which he would pay? Astoundingly, the Bodleian agreed. Even then it took five months to copy some 600 letters. For a library of such ancient reputation to be at once so stubborn, so credulous and so inefficient seems to set some sort of record for institutional atrophy. I apologize for imposing this piece of gratuitous venom on readers, but it may at least serve as useful guidance for anyone contemplating research at that library.)

But written evidence presents problems of its own, problems primarily of interpretation, all the more so when the author of the evidence is himself a writer. For a writer, at any rate one as fastidious as Amis, is always deliberate and considered in what he puts down on paper, as much in his private letters and diaries as his novels and poems. He never, ever pours out on to the page gouts of spontaneous gut feeling unfiltered or unvarnished by craft. The writer is always aware of his audience – friend, lover, fan, the public – and addresses each one in whatever form he thinks appropriate. The problem for the biographer is to disentangle these different forms of address, to gauge as best he can the various angles and distances at which the writer speaks to his diverse audiences. To read a writer's texts it is therefore a huge advantage to have first had the chance to read the writer himself.

There are any number of ways in which to interpret wrongly a writer from his writings. If, for instance, he introduces characters into his novels who drink a lot, hate 'culture,' think not much of women, gays or ethnic minorities, it is all too tempting to deduce that the writer feels and behaves in the same way. When Amis populates his fiction with characters who display such traits, and succeeds in making them vivid and credible, it is easy to ignore all the other characters who show quite different qualities and to devise a caricature of Amis as nothing more than drunk, misogynist, philistine. Someone who knows Amis well is not so likely to fall into this kind of egregious error.

For all these reasons I have come to believe that personal contact is of inestimable value to a biographer, putting the authorized variety at serious advantage over the unauthorized, in total contradiction to the balance of advantages between them I started this piece by describing. I would only qualify this by saying that the relationship between biographer and subject should be something more than the impersonal one of interviewer and interviewee. Interviews help but more is necessary.

While I was writing my book I met Amis regularly three or four times a week. We spent anything up to ten hours together, but only one or at most two of these hours were ever devoted to formal questions on matters like how he met his second wife. Most of the time could hardly be called research at all. We met at Amis's home, his local pub or the Garrick Club, sometimes just the two of us, more often with other company. During these sessions we might eat but invariably drink, quite often getting quite drunk by the finish.

If this sounds self-indulgent or amateurish, I can only ask you to believe that my informal sessions with Amis were at least as valuable as the formal ones. They helped me to read the man close up so that I could better decipher him in what he had written. This now seems to me a far more productive method than groping after the man only through texts and the erratic recollections of his friends. I suspect that anyone writing a biography of Shakespeare or Milton or any other dead or inaccessible writer would give all their teeth and hair for just one encounter with their subject. And if they don't long for such an encounter, then they should.

17

Sharing the Role: The Biographer as Sleuth

MARGARET LEWIS

The life of a crime writer has a particular fascination for the reader and offers a distinct challenge to the biographer. In general, the fictional output of a crime writer bears virtually no resemblance to the life and experience of the author. The spread-eagled bodies, the pools of blood, the intense passions that seethe until violence explodes as murder – these scenes are very far from the real lives of their creators, most of whom have never handled a gun nor entered a morgue and have no intention of doing so. Most are citizens of exemplary rectitude; the recent exposure of a popular crime writer Anne Perry, who had actually committed a murder as a young girl, rocked the crime-writing world to its core.

If the biographer is hoping to find an easy correlation between life and art, he or she is likely to be disappointed. Specialist knowledge, yes, as in the case of Dick Francis's knowledge of the race track, or Agatha Christie's basic knowledge of poisons from her work in a pharmacy, but actual experience of crime is generally absent unless the writer has been a policeman or a lawyer. Yet surely expecting to find a direct relationship between life and art is a naïve assumption that the serious student of biography will long ago have abandoned.

Depicting the life of a crime writer, if one were to be completely honest, would be to describe a strict daily routine revolving around a desk and a typewriter or word-processor. Many crime writers are reluctant to enter the social world and when they do so remain as observers, accumulating material for future use. Most of them work prodigiously hard, being bound by publishers' contracts to produce a book a year. Reginald Hill, who lives in the glorious countryside of the English Lake District, writes all week and walks or climbs on Fridays. No matter if Thursday is a superb, sunny day and Friday is pouring with rain. That is his schedule and he sticks to it.

Similarly, Ngaio Marsh used to allow herself nine months for a book (about the same as a pregnancy, she used to say) and used the remaining three to direct a production of Shakespeare in New Zealand. Agatha Christie, after one exciting moment early in her first marriage involving amnesia and a lost weekend, lived a life very much in the background as the wife of an Oxford professor, writing steadily under her own name or a pseudonym. She was extremely shy and once having been asked to arrive early at a function in her honor at the Savoy Hotel in London was nearly sent packing by an officious porter. Like Ngaio Marsh, it was the theater, not the world of books, that brought her into contact with other people.

In discussing crime writers, then, the biographer must assume from the beginning that there may be very little in the actual day-to-day life of writers to explain the kind of fiction they produce. In recent years there have been substantial biographies of the four Queens of Crime of the 1930s: Agatha Christie, Dorothy L. Sayers, Margery Allingham and Ngaio Marsh. We have learned that Agatha Christie had a fairly hum-drum existence and liked to eat cream, that Margery Allingham was badly treated by her husband, that Dorothy L. Sayers had an illegitimate child, and that Ngaio Marsh led a life divided between writing and theatre; between New Zealand and England. All these facts are interesting, but none of them help us to go very far into the creative process that involves the author casting off from a safe anchorage and launching out into the murky currents of crime.

Murky, too, are the currents surrounding psychological theories that attempt to connect crime fiction and the real world. Some writers may keep journals or diaries which reveal childhood fears or experiences that haunt their work. Ngaio Marsh, for instance, disclosed in her autobiography that she had been afraid of poisons since early childhood, after being frightened by a lurid parlor ballad sung with great gusto by her father. As a result she seldom used poison as a weapon in her novels. Agatha Christie confessed to a recurring dream that featured a threatening figure called the Gun Man. But written evidence of such childhood traumas seldom exists, and, as all biographers know, written evidence in the form of letters and journals is only as valuable as the amount of self-presentation on the part of the author that can be detected. Self-portraits and auto-biographies are always slightly suspect; there is invariably a hidden message behind the canvas or the prose.

It is more fruitful, perhaps, to look to the conventions governing crime fiction, with the emphasis on a problem and its resolution; a puzzle to be solved and a ruffled world to be set, somehow, to rights. The well-known fact that so many crime writers are crossword puzzle addicts is an indication of the way in which their minds often function, by using ingenious clues to find a pleasing and complete solution. They place much emphasis on craftsmanship in their writing: 'the writer of a thriller has no need to haul down his stylistic flag a quarter of an inch.'[1] Their intellect responds to the concept of order, yet their imaginations take them to the most extreme examples of social disorder; to violence and crime. They are particularly sensitive to the delicate membrane that quivers between harmony and lack of control in human relations. Highly observant, they often see horror in the most prosaic of household objects. They skate lightly on very thin ice above dark green depths, and take their readers safely to the other side.

The need to find a degree of order in a world of chaos may be more obvious in the detective fiction of the Golden Age, and less discernible in contemporary crime fiction. Yet even today the reader and the writer still search for a way of exploring and ordering life through fiction. P.D. James recently commented on the need to see in detective fiction a kind of logic that can be applied to human behavior:

It reaffirms our belief – or our hope – that we live in a moral and comprehensible universe in which problems can be solved by human intelligence. If we think we live in a universe that's chaotic and beyond our understanding, the more complicated the picture becomes.[2]

H.R.F. Keating agrees, suggesting that crime fiction 'can make a temporary map for its readers out of the chaos of their surroundings,'[3] and Professor John G. Cawelti in his influential study *Adventure, Mystery and Romance* states that 'the classical detective formula is perhaps the most effective fictional structure yet devised for creating the illusion of rational control over the mysteries of life.'[4]

Delving into our chaotic universe and attempting to understand it may need some particular skills on the part of the author, and some unique ammunition among the baggage wagons. In evaluating the particular qualities of crime fiction we may need to unpack some of this baggage to help us focus on the mind of the author at work. As well as considering the author's specialist knowledge, the biographer may also learn something about the writer's cast of mind by looking at the use of series characters, the adoption of pseudonyms, the significance of occasional statements by the author on his or her writing, the importance of setting, and the sense of place.

Sleuths, whether professional policemen or amateurs of one kind or another (priests, nuns and monks are surprisingly popular) may tell us more than the author intended. Dorothy L. Sayers, for instance, admitted that she had fallen in love with the suave and handsome Lord Peter Wimsey. Ngaio Marsh, who never married, invented Detective Chief Inspector Roderick Alleyn who might well have swept her off her feet; and a character, Agatha Troy, a tall, lanky painter who was not dissimilar to herself in looks or personality. For Arthur Conan Doyle, struggling in a failing medical practice in Southsea, the creation of a superman who could solve all problems was irresistible. That this particular character was a cocaine addict and a flamboyant depressive as well as what Julian Symons called 'a Nietzschean superior man'[5] simply indicated the extent of Conan Doyle's artistic range. Sara Paretsky, who was very active in feminist politics in the 1970s, has produced a popular and enduring character in her female private eye, V.I. Warshawski. Here is a role model for the late twentieth century, not quite a superman but someone who uses today's ratiocinative methods (generally involving the use of computer-based records) to help her friends and nudge a little justice into under-privileged lives. Women in particular respond to this super-confident heroine, just as earlier readers were captivated by the competence of Holmes.

But even if series characters may suggest something about the author's attitude towards life, there is still no satisfactory answer to the fundamental dichotomy between the violence of crime fiction and the blameless life of the author. As Ngaio Marsh mused in her auto-biography *Black Beech and Honeydew*:

People sometimes remark on the gruesomeness of some of the murders in my earlier books and are inclined to take the line of wondering how a nice old dear like me could dream up such beastliness, let alone write about it. The idea being, I fancy, that perhaps the old dear is not so nice after all. I really have no answer to this . . . with the deepest respect to the psychiatrists, I really don't think I'm sublimating any bloody inclinations lurking in my unconscious or id or libido or whatever it is and if that's the right way of putting it. I am, in fact, extremely squeamish. . . .[6]

P.D. James is equally non-committal, saying that, 'We are interested in the details of living. Whether or not we also have a lot of hidden aggression which we are sublimating, I wouldn't want to say.'[7]

Of course it can be argued that any creative writer must of necessity possess a vivid imagination in order to create characters, cause them to inhabit a setting and develop a credible tale. What makes crime writers unique is the fact that their fiction is shaped by violent crimes which they describe in detail and examine many times over, so many times that the reader is distanced from the cruelty and suffering depicted. The formula distances not only the reader, but the practitioner, something that was grasped by Thomas de Quincey as early as 1827, when in his essay 'On Murder Considered as One of the Fine Arts' he wrote:

> People begin to see something more goes to the composition of a fine murder than two blockheads to kill and be killed – a knife – a purse – and a dark lane. Design, gentlemen, grouping, light and shade, poetry, sentiment, are now deemed indispensable to attempts of this nature.[8]

Although de Quincey's witty essay deals with the actual fact of murder, and gives several examples, his description of the style of the deed has a lot to tell us about the way in which the craft of crime fiction has developed.

Ngaio Marsh was certainly devoted to the notion of design and form in her work. Yet although she may have claimed to be squeamish, her murders were vicious and she researched them very thoroughly. One of her most gruesome murders, in *Scales of Justice*, involves a woman killing her husband by striking his head with a golf club as he sits fishing on a riverbank, and then impaling his head with the pointed end of a shooting stick. This crime involved considerable empirical study on the part of the writer. Ngaio invited a friend, a retired police inspector, to join her on the terrace so that they could impale a selection of melons and judge the amount of force necessary to pierce a man's temple. She caused a skewer to be driven through the victim's eye in *Surfeit of Lampreys* (published as *Death of a Peer* in the United States) having taken precise medical advice on ways to ensure an efficient death. A bullet through the head would have been an easy death for one of Miss Marsh's victims.

The clash between good and evil is now seldom part of a crime writer's vocabulary as increasingly shades of gray have become more interesting to readers; the question of 'whodunit' becoming less significant than 'why.' Ellis Peters (pseudonym of Edith Pargeter) is one writer who has not shirked the need to define these terms. Peters has written over ninety books of various kinds – histories, contemporary detective novels, adventures, romances, translations and, most successfully, the chronicles of Brother Cadfael. Now aged over eighty, she continues a writing career begun in the 1930s when she left school to work in a local pharmacy near her home in Shropshire. She had a demanding but exhilarating period of war service in the WRNS, the Women's Royal Naval Service, producing one novel directly out of that experience and a war-time trilogy set on various battlefields that taxed her literary imagination to the utmost. Shortly after the war she visited Czechoslovakia with her brother, Ellis, and from that time regular visits to her friends there formed an important focus for her life and interests. The rest of her time was spent at her desk, writing. Her output was phenomenal; in a single year she was capable of producing a contemporary detective novel, an historical novel and a Czech translation.

Edith Pargeter remains a very private individual and has said that she does not want a biography written about her. The book about her life and work that she permitted in 1994 reveals very little about her personal circumstances except for her love of Czechoslovakia, of music and of history. The biographer can, however, take from all her work a profound sense of morality. She has said:

> Apart from treating my characters with the same respect as in any other form of novel, I have one sacred rule about the thriller. It is, it must be, a morality. If it strays from the side of the angels, provokes total despair, wilfully destroys – without pressing need in the plot – the innocent and the good, takes pleasure in evil, that is unforgivable sin. I use the word deliberately and gravely.[9]

Edith has given much thought to the role of human beings in society and her idiosyncratic hero, Brother Cadfael, rules his conduct by an innate sense of justice and humanity as well as faith. He, like Sherlock Holmes, can feel it right for criminals to escape occasionally, and to respond to the more mottled shades of gray instead of black and white. Raymond Chandler's hero, Philip Marlowe, also understood this situation very well.

The creation of series characters is particularly important for crime writers and again, an understanding of the eugenics of the genre is useful here. Publishers are fond of series characters and often put a great deal of pressure on writers to keep them going. They offer contracts for several books over a number of years which can effectively bind the writer in chains if he or she is not careful. Attempts by the author to escape can be drastic, as when Doyle pushed his hero off the Reichenbach Falls. Unhappily for Doyle he was recaptured as he raced off into the heady air of historical fiction and was dragged back to his desk by an indignant nation. Other writers find themselves backed into awkward corners as a series goes on much longer than expected, and heroes such as Hercule Poirot (whom Agatha eventually found 'insufferable') and Roderick Alleyn remain fresh and young when logically they ought to be nearly a hundred years old. Instead they inhabit a rather hazy time-warp which gets further and further from reality as the series drags on.

Like anyone with a murky past, the crime writer often finds that the only way to bound free is to create a new character and a new identity. Pseudonyms are commonly used in genre fiction and readers are often surprised to find that men write energetically as women, women write as men, and some remain indefinable. A change of name can indicate a change of approach or quite a different type of fiction. The most notable example is John Creasey, who managed to write 560 novels using more than twenty pseudonyms, all representing slightly different aspects of the genre. More recently, Ruth Rendell writing as Barbara Vine produces novels that concentrate much more on the psychological interaction of criminal and victim than on the procedures of police work that drive her other books. Ellis Peters chose male pseudonyms for her early crime books (Jolyon Carr, John Redfern) and kept her own name, Edith Pargeter, for non-crime novels, translations and histories. The Ellis Peters pseudonym did not appear until 1959 and was retained for the Felse novels and the Cadfael Chronicles after that.

Sometimes old-fashioned views of 'serious' as opposed to genre fiction affect a decision to use a pseudonym. Poet Laureate Cecil Day-Lewis wrote his 'tecs as Nicholas Blake and the distinguished scholar and critic Professor J.I.M. Stewart led a double life as crime writer Michael Innes for many years. Julian Symons rather mischievously suggests that:

> The essence of crime stories is that they conceal something, and it is psychologically appropriate that the author's identity should also be hidden. Is it going too far to suggest that through use of a pseudonym writers are able to indulge secret thoughts, and write about subjects which they would otherwise have found it difficult to approach?[10]

The more interesting question, perhaps, and one that puzzled me a great deal in writing the biography of Ngaio Marsh, is why talented writers do not more often attempt to become established as literary novelists. The answer is seldom straightforward and may turn us again to the special features of the crime fiction genre. The formula, no matter how lightly applied, is still a protective coat. A different kind of novel is bound to reveal more about the individual author, no matter how many personae are launched upon the stage. Furthermore, the publishing world tends to place artificial fences around certain types of books, and attempts by fine writers such as P.D. James and Julian Symons to have their crime novels treated as seriously as any other kind of novel about the human condition have, even now, not been totally successful.

Consideration of setting and place may well give more clues than anything else about our author's world, but even this is not always the case. H.R.F. Keating had set several of his Inspector Ghote novels in India before he finally made his first visit there. Ngaio Marsh set only four of her thirty-two novels in New Zealand although she lived there almost all her life, in the house where she grew up. Many writers carry out concentrated research to support a particular approach; others do just enough to convince the reader that the author's knowledge of Kathmandu, the Kalahari Desert or the Hidden City of Beijing is the result of long years of intimacy with the most subtle details of the location. That being said, many writers acquire a very particular flavor from immediate experience of their landscapes. Tony Hillerman's evocative descriptions of the Navajo people on the reservations of south-western America, for instance, or Arthur Upfield's unforgettable descriptions of the Australian outback, or Ellis Peters's firm settings on the Welsh borders and her depiction of the craftsmen of Shrewsbury, are essential to the workings of their plots.

The biographer appears to be doing rather badly as far as evidence goes. It seems that the writer, self-sufficient and in control, sits at his or her desk in a well-appointed study producing at least an annual novel. The exercise is entirely cerebral and does not involve much more than stretching an arm out to various reference books to check up on such tricky problems as bruising, knife entry points and poisons. Nothing up to now has told the inquisitive and increasing desperate biographer *why* the author selected that particular genre or why he or she continues happily doing the shopping or mowing the lawn while working out the details of a particularly violent murder. Can it really be simply the lure of a lucrative contract, or the conviction that they can do as well or better than the latest mystery that they have just thrown aside?

Biographical sleuths may indeed often feel that they are taking over the role of the investigating officer as they seek out the clues, interview witnesses and evaluate evidence. Danger arises, as in a genuine criminal investigation, when evidence is manipulated, given undue prominence or even suppressed in order to support a theory imposed from outside, rather than allowing the truth to emerge. When all is said and done, any literary biography has as its subject a solitary individual sitting in a chair, facing a blank piece of paper. Imagination, craftsmanship and hard work do the rest, together with the ingredient that is hardest of all to define or describe, the spark of creativity. For many people, and perhaps crime writers fall into this category more readily than others, the quick-silver life of the imagination is immeasurably more satisfying than any life that the real world can offer. No amount of carefully assembled detail can obscure the fact that it is the world of the imagination that matters.

18

Reflections of a Biographer

ELIZABETH LONGFORD

Inspiration comes to biographers as much as to novelists but cannot be commanded by any cerebral tricks. Nevertheless one can do something to help it breathe.

In the last twenty years, I have worked out a 'writing day' for myself. I write best in the morning, though not immediately after breakfast. I use that first hour to write letters or shopping lists; even the laundry list loosens me up and gets me going with a pen. Writing out-of-doors suits me best, either in the Sussex garden or on the Chelsea balcony. Outdoor sounds seem to absorb the distractive parts of my brain and leave the rest free to concentrate. It may be that I have got used over the years to writing in some degree of noise indoors: children in the same room or myself on a train journey. The only place I can't perform is at a desk on a straight-backed chair. Writing late at night seems more inspirational than it is. I seldom find the results come up to scratch when I reread them next morning. Indeed, problems that appear insoluble at midnight have a way of smoothly solving themselves at midday.

Structure and chronology are among the perennial problems. How to deal with the subject's personal and public life? They happen simultaneously, whereas in the biography there may have to be some measure of separation. Should it be separate chapters? Or separate sections within the same chapter? I have used both methods, though the former more with public male characters who tend, conveniently for the biographer, to compartmentalize their lives. Women, even public women, are more 'open plan.'

I reread endlessly what I have written and make continual corrections: sometimes substantial ones involving rearrangements of material, more often verbal changes. Really obstinate problems have to be solved with the help of manual labor – preferably gardening. Clearing the ground for a rosebush clears away the mental rubbish as well.

All these techniques to be developed for what? Biography. Not for the (superior) arts of fiction or history. I think biography chose me, as it chooses most of its operators. And chose me because I wanted to write in the ways it had to offer. Michael Holroyd, author of *Lytton Strachey*, has said that biography is the nearest art to the novel. It is about people, and it thrives on imagination, to decipher them if not to create. I prefer to work on people who were or are *there*, as a doctor or teacher does, not so much on might-have-beens. I like to see them in my mind's eye as a novelist does, but also to see the actual letters they wrote, the clothes they wore. There is a special excitement in handling their possessions that seems to generate extra perceptiveness.

I like my subject to be encapsulated in a life, as history is not. All the same, my biographies must always to some extent be a 'Life and Times of. . . .' The balance between 'Life' and 'Times,' however, is one of the most difficult to achieve. A reviewer said there was not enough historical background in my first biography (*Queen Victoria*); when I tried to repair that omission in my second (*Wellington*), another reviewer said there was too much. Can one win? Help has come, notwithstanding, from two guidelines, the first offered by Cecil Woodham-Smith, biographer of Florence Nightingale: 'Always keep your narrative moving.' That means, among other things, avoidance of too much argument with other historians, a pastime in which academics delight. My second rule is never to lose sight of my subject for more than a page or so. I aim at the maximum of background detail with the minimum of digression.

Another elusive question of balance concerns sympathy with one's subject. I could never write a biography of, say, Hitler, though I recognize the need for such works; perhaps the author's righteous indignation supplies the adrenaline usually produced by enthusiasm. Every self-respecting biographer tries to avoid hagiography like a plague of treacle.

Perhaps the thing I am really striving for is empathy. While sympathy merely means fellow feeling, empathy means 'the power of projecting one's personality into, and fully understanding, the object of contemplation.' I can do this only with someone I like.

Incidentally, the one thing that makes biography unreadable is to lecture or rebuke one's subject.

Detection is another aspect of biography that I like: both the probing into character and the weighing up of fact versus legend. A Catch-22 situation is often involved at the beginning of these researches. If one reads secondary sources first – other authors' books – one may be prejudiced by them before one has had time to form one's own opinion; but if one goes straight into the original sources – letters and diaries – one may not be sufficiently well equipped to detect the hidden evidence on some controversy or problem. My own solution has been to read (or reread) *one* general account first and then dive into the primary sources.

Questions of fact or legend require exhaustive research but are sometimes solved by accident, occasionally too late, alas, for one's current book. I could not decide, for example, whether Queen Elizabeth II kept a real diary or merely a brief engagement record. After the publication of *The Queen*, I happened to mention this doubt during a lecture to a conference of American university women in London. One of them came up to me and said: 'I *know*. When our group was introduced to her Majesty, I asked: "Ma'am, do you keep a diary? If so, how do you find the time?" The Queen replied, "Prince Philip and Prince Charles read in bed. I write my diary. And it's a great deal more honest than anything you'll find in the media".'

In the decade when I became a biographer – the 1960s – a double revolution in the art took place, the matrix being American universities. First, the availability of sources suddenly increased with the large-scale collecting of archives and the development of photocopying.

Second came the distinction between narrative and analytical–psychological biography. While I myself did not abandon narrative, I have learned from the disciplines of in-depth research. Forget all we ever knew about biography from *The Oxford Dictionary of Quotations*, especially Disraeli's 'Read no history: nothing but biography, for that is life without theory.' Today in certain quarters biography has become theory without life. As far as possible, the life *story* is ignored; even dates of birth and death may be hard to find. There is instead a wealth of interpretation of the subject's own words, which should eventually lay bare the naked self, the 'inner me.' Individual lives being incoherent, there must be no attempt at continuous narrative but everything should be 'discontinuous' and open-ended.

In still safeguarding narrative, I accept the need to add to my duties as biographer the roles of interpreter, mediator between other writers' views, and analyst. My chief fear is that the analytical game may become too facile, too seductive.

Biography is too important to become a playground for fantasies, however ingenious; I believe its future is safe with the reading public, who will keep it human, not too solemn.

19

The Biographer's Revenge *

JOHN HALPERIN

A poet's life is his work.

Tennessee Williams

I

In his essay entitled 'What Is an Author?,' Michel Foucault reduces the teller of tales from a person to an adjective. The high priest of post-modernism refers not to the author but rather to 'the author function'; 'What does it matter who is speaking?' he asks. The author, he says, is 'the dead man in the game of writing.'

The structuralists, Roland Barthes especially, declared that the task of criticism was not to elucidate the relationship of the work to the author, nor to analyze the work through the author's thought or experience, but rather to analyze the work through its structure alone – its architecture, its intrinsic form, and the play of its linguistic relationships. Post-modernism invents the death and disappearance of the author, circumvents references to him or her, and ignores both the act of writing and the possible meanings the author may have wished to express. Post-modernists attempt to imagine the general condition of a text – the space in which it is dispersed and the time in which it unfolds. They go beyond the affirmation that the author is both invisible and irrelevant and try to locate and describe the space left empty by his death, to follow the distribution of gaps caused by

*Two different versions of this essay, from which the present one has been revised and updated, appeared, respectively, in *Journal of Australasian Universities Language and Literature Association*, LXIX (1988), and *Biography*, XII (1989).

his disappearance, and to look for the openings his disappearance has uncovered.

Since the author has ceased to exist, why not, Foucault asks, remove his name altogether from the work? A private letter, a legal contract, an anonymous message posted on the wall may have a signer, a guarantor, or a composer – but none of these 'texts,' Foucault argues, has an author. In the same way, literary works should be treated as if they were anonymous. The whole idea of authorship, Foucault concludes, is only a projection made by readers.

Despite his demise, the author remains for Foucault potentially 'a great peril, the great danger with which fiction threatens our world.' We must, he declares, 'entirely reverse the traditional idea of the author.' For the author, he argues, does not 'precede' his own work: 'he is a certain fictional principle' which may force readers to limit, exclude, and – worst horror of all – choose meanings: the author, Foucault says, 'impedes the free circulation, the free manipulation, the free composition, decomposition, and recomposition of fiction.' In other words, the author is an inconvenience the critic would do well to ignore. The author of a novel, according to Foucault, is only an 'ideological product' or figure which interferes with 'the proliferation of meaning.' Acknowledging his existence reduces the number of interpretative paths the critic may wish to take. Ultimately, Foucault prophesies, the whole idea, the whole concept of authorship will disappear along with the author, thus allowing the critic a clear, uncluttered route to 'polysemous' texts which can be 'experienced' without any reference to their authorship. Foucault hopes that all texts may finally envelop themselves in what he calls 'the anonymity of a murmur.' He does not after all wish to know 'who is speaking,' or which parts of his deepest self the author expresses in what he writes. Since an author can speak neither with authenticity nor originality, 'What difference does it make,' Foucault asks, 'who is speaking?'

The deconstructionists argue that language by its very nature is circular and can refer only to itself, never to anything outside itself. Do words, deconstructionists want to know, refer to things, to other words, or to both? Because, they say, the language of a text can refer only to other languages and other texts and never to some tangible extratextual entity, the work as a whole can always have a multiplicity of meanings, which may wind up undermining one another, becoming irreconcilable, rendering 'meaning' impossible to locate and thus, ultimately, irrelevant. This is an idea they like. Taken to the extreme, the text can be seen as immolating itself in multiple meanings. Readings of texts are everything, authors and the texts they have actually produced are nothing. Language ceases to be a product of taste or historical usage, and becomes instead simply a metaphor – or, rather, a metaphor about metaphors – finally not only unknowable but also unparaphrasable. The reader becomes more important than either the author or the text and is left alone to make the text mean anything he likes. Thus the critic J. Hillis Miller actually says somewhere that 'there is not any Shakespeare. . . . "Shakespeare" is an effect of the text.' But Oscar Wilde is likelier to be right when he declares that 'it is because [Shakespeare] never speaks to us of himself in his plays that his plays reveal him to us absolutely, and show us his true nature and temperament.'

As the deconstructionists treat language, it can never mean anything. They are willing to give us, from time to time, examples of their method. Here is one. In the phrase, 'Do you see my point?,' a feminist deconstructionist, according to the critic Murray Krieger, would argue that the words used undermine the speaker's purpose, since the figure of speech contains phallic symbolism. I can only suppose that a gay male deconstructionist given to fencing as a pastime might take another meaning from 'Do you see my point?' Surely the literary critic's profession is to elucidate, rather than to make impenetrable, the process by which ordinary people interact with their own language. Do you see my point?

According to the deconstructionists, we are not only unable to determine what words mean; we are unable, finally, to know what words are. Taken to their logical extreme, the deconstructionists can be seen as arguing that it is pointless to read, because we can never know what we are reading.

Deconstruction's high priests tell us that any work can be deconstructed. Jacques Derrida, the arch-boa-deconstructor of this dead system, is fond of deconstructing, for exercise, the Declaration of Independence. Hillis Miller, who has said that he speaks a language that speaks through him, explains that the phrase 'We the people' in the Declaration of Independence has 'no reference in reality,' since the people did not exist until they were first defined in that document. The sad fact – and deconstructionists tend to find facts generally depressing – is that the phrase 'We the people' occurs not in the Declaration of Independence but rather in the Preamble to the Constitution of the United States; if the phrase brings with it 'no reference in reality' to Professor Miller, this may be one reason why. In fact, as any historian could tell you, the concept of 'the people' existed long before either the Declaration of Independence or the US

Constitution. The Greek noun 'demos' means 'the people,' and so does the Latin word 'populus,' from which, as a matter of fact, the word 'people' comes. The phrase 'Senatus Populusque Romanus' – abbreviated to 'SPQR' – was inscribed on the standards of the Roman armies and can still be found today, legible enough for even a deconstructionist to read, on many ancient Italian buildings. But the deconstructionists are not interested in history, which they are fond of describing as narrative stories, like novels. Thus a deconstructionist would feel uncomfortable having to make a generic distinction between, say, Lady Longford's *Queen Victoria* and Wilkie Collins' *The Woman in White*, or between *The Joy of Cooking* and *Naked Lunch*.

Another instance of deconstruction's unwise contempt for historical fact may be found in Derrida's account of Plato's account of the death of Socrates. Derrida argues that Plato's use of the Greek word 'pharmakos,' which he says means both 'remedy' and 'poison,' is one proof that the meaning of Plato's work is ultimately 'undecidable.' The word Plato actually uses is not 'pharmakos' but rather 'pharmakon,' which does indeed mean both 'remedy' and 'poison,' as Plato meant it to. Plato and his contemporary audience, one feels certain, had as good a command of fifth-century Greek as Derrida, and when Plato called the hemlock which Socrates drank 'pharmakon' they knew perfectly well what he meant without having to deconstruct his language. 'Pharmakos,' I am happy to report, means neither 'remedy' nor 'poison' but rather 'scapegoat,' or sacrificial offering to the gods to cure some human ailment.

For Jacques Lacan, another leading light of post-modernism, writers are little more than deluded animals through whom, during hours of unconscious madness, images and compulsions accidentally get put into words.

Deconstruction is a form of escapism, an attempt to demolish traditional values and meanings, along with such concepts as social contracts and laws of nature, in order not to have to deal with them. There was life before Derrida, and there will be life after him. Derrida, Foucault, Lacan, Barthes: the French have a lot to answer for. Structuralism and post-structuralism have had the effect of blurring, and attempting to erase, all generic distinctions, so that the Declaration of Independence (when it really is the Declaration of Independence and not something else) can be read in the same way as *Paradise Lost* or *The Ambassadors*, denying to literature any connection with reality and ultimately rejecting the inconvenient idea that there are good and bad interpretations of a work.

Frederick C. Crews has commented on what he calls the new 'theoreticism.' The major shift we have witnessed over the past generation, Crews argues in *Skeptical Engagements*, his brilliant commentary on contemporary criticism, is not a growing taste for big ideas but a growing apriorism, a willingness to settle issues by theoretical decree without even a pretense of evidential appeal. In 1960 nearly everyone would have concurred with R.S. Crane's observation that one of the most important marks of the good scholar is a habitual distrust of the *a priori*; that is to say, of all ways of arriving at particular conclusions which assume the relevance and authority, prior to the concrete evidence, of theoretical doctrines or other general propositions. But today, as Crews says, we are surrounded by theoreticism: frank recourse to unsubstantiated theory, not just as a tool of investigation but as anti-empirical knowledge in its own right. Crews reminds us that Geoffrey Hartman, a disciple of Derrida, admits in his book *Saving the Text* that he has no interest in the relation of theory to empirical evidence. Hartman, Crews points out, appears to believe that the only significant literary *genre* of our day is criticism itself and to advocate the cultivation in the critic of an exquisite vagueness. The very idea of acquiring definite knowledge of literature, of considering facts of any kind, takes on in his mind the status of a national emergency.

Foucault's epistemology rules out the concept of a fact. In his book *Madness and Civilization*, in which Foucault – rightly, in my opinion – claims to be speaking on behalf of madness, this Professor Moriarty of post-modernism says that he wants his books to be Molotov cocktails that will self-destruct after use. This violent imagery, Crews reminds us, is typical of theoreticism, which, in the way of all totalitarian systems, refuses to credit its audience with the right to challenge ideas dispassionately. It wishes to conquer, not to debate. It is no coincidence, surely, that so many of the French critics, as well as their disciples in America and Britain, have tended to include in their circle of deconstructionist deities the late Martin Heidegger, one of Hitler's earliest supporters. Make no mistake about it, deconstruction is fascism: other points of view will not be tolerated. Between 1940 and 1942 Paul de Man wrote and published nearly 200 articles for pro-Nazi collaborationist newspapers and periodicals in Belgium. Many of these took as their theme the 'pollution' of literature by Jewish writers. In one of his many anti-Semitic pieces, the late, unlamented one declares that Jewish writers are mediocrities whose deportation *en masse* would not injure European culture.' A leopard cannot change its spots,' de Man says here. 'Jews are Asiatics; they are a menace to the nation that admits them, and they should be excluded.' 'Hitlerism,' he observes in another article, promises 'the definitive emancipation of a people that finds itself called upon to exercise hegemony in Europe.' As David Lehman has written, deconstruction, of which de Man was one of the great arch-deacons, has always disturbed those who value humanism precisely because it refuses to make any provision in literature for moral action, or for the actions, moral or otherwise, of authors. It would be poetically just, as Lehman observes, if so anti-biographical a theory of literature should ultimately be vanquished by the discovery of ruinous biographical facts about its gurus. Fascist in his politics, de Man, the Kurt Waldheim of post-modernism, found in deconstruction a soothingly amoral, anti-humanistic approach to art which suited him temperamentally and which in fact typifies most deconstructive commentaries.

When the French structuralist Louis Althusser strangled his wife in 1980, he was judged mentally incompetent to stand trial. I cannot help wondering how many of his disciples could pass the same test today. Like Foucault's ideal critic, theorists are prone to self-destruct after use. Some of them go on to other trendy schools of thought, and some of them, apparently, are incarcerated for society's protection. Is it pure coincidence, I wonder, that at the time he murdered his wife Althusser was undergoing psychoanalysis at the hands of Jacques Lacan? Lacan allowed his patients exactly five minutes per visit; obviously Althusser needed more time. Has a whole generation of critics gone mad? In their desire to destroy meanings and identities, the post-modernists are concerned only with the explosions they may cause: remember Foucault's Molotov cocktail. Indeed, some contemporary post-modernists remind me of the Hungarian murderer Sylvestre Matuschka, who could experience sexual excitement only when he saw trains crashing, and caused dramatic railway collisions to arouse himself.

II

The concern which seems to me to justify the profession of criticism, the concern which can, at times, enable the critic to make for his own contemporaries a contribution to the elucidation of classic literature, is not the study of the relation of the component parts of a text to one another, but rather the study of the historical and biographical milieux in which texts are brought into being and by which their nature is determined: the study of the relation, to put it plainly, of art to life. What may help us to understand what we read is the admission that the connections between literature and the cultural moment at which it is composed, and by which its shape is moulded, are both inevitable and comprehensible, both 'decidable' and explainable.

I am not interested in criticism which allegedly reveals to us what the text is composed of without attempting to explain why it has been composed in that fashion. Every creative act appears to me to have its origin in the confluence of the artist and the moment; and while texts can be ingeniously and tediously deconstructed to yield up some of their component parts and to show some of the ways in which these parts are related to one another, such a self-limiting critical approach strikes me as nihilistic, ultimately amoral. Post-modernists treat literature in the same way in which physicists treat particles: as soulless things to be watched. The post-modern critic is not interested in what literature is, or even in what it says – but only in how it looks. He has the soul of a maitre d'.

I think language is always employed intentionally: that is, the writer when he writes intends to say something particular and specific. The author always means something. Language does not speak; people do. The meaning of a text is the author's meaning, not the critic's, and it can be shared by the reader. If you don't believe this, why read? The critic's job is, and has always been, to find out the author's meaning, not to search his own psyche for the meaning the author forgot to give us. The hermeneutic nihilists who believe, as Derrida puts it, that black marks on white paper constitute a text, and that meaning is forever 'not yet,' are guilty of what I would call absurdist terrorism. More significantly, these people are guilty of a great be-trayal: in their rush to de-mean meaning they want to take away not only the joy of reading but the relevance of the humanities and of humanistic studies to our own lives.

Let us address ourselves further to this question of meaning. Is meaning always inaccessible or undiscoverable? Different critics may find different meanings in the same work, and yet each of these meanings may be mutually inclusive: that is, each interpretation or reading, different though it may be from the others, might be plausible (and thus 'right') because it can be supported in some way by the manner in which we apprehend the text. The primary function of literary criticism must still be an attempt to tell us what literature means, or what it might mean. And if you believe this, then inevitably you come back again and again not to the reader but to the author as the paramount and the most permanent and reliable source of meaning, for it is always within the author's personality and the author's point of view, shaped by forces not always undiscoverable, that keys to meaning can be found; whereas each reader, as the post-modernists admit and demonstrate, brings to the text his own highly personal perspective. Meaning, when it can be located, is found in authors, not in critics. Criticism itself has no meaning.

By focusing on the reader's collision with the text as the significant subject to be addressed by the critic, Frederick Crews reminds us, the post-modernists have attempted to turn literary criticism into something entirely subjective and onanistic; for them, meaning, if it exists anywhere, exists not in the text but rather within the critic himself, revealed by the critical methodology he uses. Thus criticism becomes its own end, and the critic rather than the author or the text becomes the focus and the subject of criticism. Meaning is seen to reside in the critic rather than the author. In fact, the critic becomes the author. The author's place is usurped by the critic, who by this means makes the author appear to disappear. What the critic does is considered the only source of meaning in a critical system which declares that meaning is impossible to locate anywhere outside itself. As Crews says, the post-modernists are guilty not only of murdering the author; they are guilty as well of trying to put themselves in his place. They are the Claudiuses of criticism. The critic asks us to study himself and what he does rather than the author and what he does, or the text and what it actually says. Literature gets lost in the search for the critic and the key to his method. The critic becomes his own subject, the author dies, and courses in critical theory replace courses in literature in the academic curriculum.

Stanley Fish, the highest priest of reader-response theory, is perhaps the most notorious practitioner of this expiring system. He has written that the dismissal of objectivity in literary criticism relieves the critic of the obligation to be right and demands only that he be interesting. In *Surprised by Sin*, Professor Fish claims that Milton wanted us to misread his elaborately suspended sentences, forming premature conclusions as we struggle from phrase to phrase, so that he could repeatedly surprise us and thereby remind us of our fallen state. But if this was indeed Milton's aim, the real surprise, as Crews observes in *Skeptical Engagements*, is that it went unnoticed for 300 years and was then discovered by one reader.

I mind less the deconstructionists questioning of whether or not departments of literature ought to exist than I mind the assumption many of them make that there is no such thing as literature, since it cannot be defined satisfactorily in their terms, and that therefore no formal mechanism for studying it, in a way which may bring pleasure and enjoyment to many people, can exist. Of course it is nonsense to say that there is no such thing as literature; it is much more likely that there is no such thing as post-modernism. One recalls Proust's reference to 'the fatal progress of aestheticism which ends by eating its own tail.' Near the end of *Le temps retrouvé* he goes on to make an observation which would seem to be of special relevance here.

Plenty of people who lack the artistic sense, who lack . . . the faculty of submitting to the reality within themselves . . . may possess the ability to expatiate upon the theory of art until the crack of doom. . . . They are likely to believe that literature is an intellectual game destined in the future to be progressively eliminated. Their literary 'theories' seem to me to indicate very clearly the inferiority of those who uphold them. . . . Authentic art has no use for proclamations . . . it accomplishes its work in silence. Moreover, those who theorize . . . use hackneyed phrases which [have] a curious resemblance to those of the idiots whom they denounce.

III

To ignore the author, as if he were not responsible for what he produces out of nothing, as if the madness of artistic creation overtakes him every time he picks up a pen and goes into a Lacanian trance during which words somehow land on the page, as if by magic, surely is naïve. Such a perspective betrays ignorance of how artists actually function. How can we separate the dancer from the dance? All artists, even bad ones, are conscious to some extent of what they do, whether they do what they think they intended to do or not. Nor can any writer, even if it occurred to him to try to do so, escape from the historical moment or the envelope of personality out of which his creativity emerges. Literary criticism as practiced by the post-modernists, and in becoming largely autobiographical, has also become, in a sense, another kind of fiction – that is, something made up, a game with no rules, while attention to the historical and biographical properties of art are deliberately excluded.

The text is a product of what the writer is and what he thinks; no writer writes without reference to self, consciously or not; no writer can live in a time other than his own. So long as we have his work in front of us, how can the author possibly be dead? Removing his name from the title-page, as Foucault suggests, changes nothing. I notice that Foucault and his brethren share no impulse to remove their own names from the title-pages of their books. When they write, apparently it does matter 'who is speaking.'

In his biography of Joyce, the late Richard Ellmann has written:

> The life of an artist . . . differs from the lives of other persons in that its events are becoming artistic sources even as they command his present attention. Instead of allowing each day, pushed back by the next, to lapse into imprecise memory, he shapes again the experiences which have shaped him. He is at once the captive and the liberator. In turn the process of reshaping experience becomes a part of his life, another of its recurrent events like rising or sleeping. The biographer must measure in each moment this participation of the artist in two simultaneous processes.

One might say this another way: we must study the artist in order to know the work.

I do not mean to suggest that biography can be an exact science, always purely factual. A disclaimer is necessary here: biographies are as good or as bad as the biographers who write them. It is inevitable that a biography, like any other written work, must also in part be autobiographical. 'When a man is attempting to describe another's character,' Coleridge wrote in his Notebook, 'he may be right or he may be wrong – but in one thing he will always succeed, in describing *himself*.' In fact Thomas Hardy tried to write his own biography, signing to it, as its author, the name of his second wife – who, as soon as he was dead, excised from it everything favorable about the first Mrs Hardy. The various versions of Hardy's life produced by this writing team, this Mr and Mrs Hardy, comprise an interesting piece of fiction but hardly a biography. Oscar Wilde declared that 'the only portraits in which one believes are portraits where there is very little of the sitter and a very great deal of the artist.' This formula was faithfully followed by Lytton Strachey when he came to write *Eminent Victorians*, which is largely about his own attitudes to his grandfathers' generation and bears little resemblance to the truth about the four subjects he addresses there. Strachey did not perform brilliantly as a student of history at Cambridge, and in a sense his books constitute the revenge he took upon the university examiners who gave him only a second-class degree in the historical tripos.

In his superb commentary on the science of biography, *Biography: Fiction, Fact, and Form*, Ira B. Nadel puts it this way. Most biographers understand that facts by themselves are not enough to constitute a reliable Life – that they may be manipulated, selected, omitted, or forgotten in the telling of the biographer's story. The bad biographer may alter or eliminate facts if they happen not to coincide with his idea of his subject: the best example I can think of is Michael Millgate's life of Hardy. The good biographer will try to guarantee the accuracy, the reliability, and the relevance of whatever facts he chooses to present to the reader – and 'chooses' is the operative word here, because all biographies necessarily are miniatures, comprising the choice of facts the biographer has made. There is always some sort of relationship, friendly or unfriendly, rarely neutral, between the biographer and his subject – or between the artist and the sitter, to use Wilde's terms.

The identification of and interaction between the biographer and the biographee may occur on any of several levels, as Professor Nadel has observed. The chief of these is the historical; if the biographer actually knew the subject – e.g., Elizabeth Gaskell and Charlotte Brontë – she will not be able to avoid including in her account her own view of things. The biographer who finds intrusion into her own narrative inevitable will usually wish that this was not possible, and that the rule of what I like to call 'The Deader the Better' is the safest for any would-be biographer to follow. As Proust says, 'On the whole . . . the wisest thing is to stick to dead authors. . . . A dead writer can be illustrious without any strain on himself.' Distance makes objectivity more likely. Of course Hardy could not write about himself truthfully; of course Strachey could not write without prejudice of a generation he hated. Stymied by the conflict between what she knew at firsthand about Roger Fry's personality and her research into the facts of his life, Virginia Woolf, as Ira Nadel reminds us, produced a wooden, inert biography of her friend and mentor. 'How can one cut loose from the facts when there they are, contradicting my theories,' she complained in her Diary.

Does the recognition that biography may be both creative and autobiographical mean that it must always be unreliable, no less fictional than a deconstructionist commentary? Does the necessary presence of the biographer in his work, as undeniable as the presence of the novelist in his work, undermine the authenticity of biography? Is biography indistinguishable from fiction, and are the postmodernists right in their refusal to distinguish between *genres* or to care 'who is speaking'? Are *The Joy of Cooking* and *Naked Lunch* the same book after all?

Assuming that the biographer is worthy of his profession, the answer must always be 'No.' Biographers, Professor Nadel observes, perceive the disorderly nature of the life they are writing about and the imperfections of their form; the best of them try to make some order and completeness out of the chaos anyone's life must be. The biographer has before him a bundle of letters: which should he quote from? He selects a letter: which parts of it should be quoted? The 'good' biographer makes choices which as far as possible are objective rather than propagandistic or self-serving. The 'bad' biographer, knowing that anything can be proved if enough is omitted, quotes from those private papers only what he wishes his readers to see.

In his life of Proust, George D. Painter declares: 'The biographer's task ... is to ... discover, beneath the mask of the artist's every-day, objective life, the secret life from which he extracted his work; show how, in the apparently sterile persons and places of that external life, he found the hidden, universal meanings which are the themes of his book; and reveal the drama of the contrast and interaction between his daily existence and his immeasurably deeper life as a creator.' As we have seen, in his life of Joyce, Richard Ellmann says pretty much the same thing. One's standards for biography must not be impossibly high. In *Biography: Fiction, Fact, and Form*, Ira Nadel reminds us that the reader of a biography should try to remember that he is dealing with a written rather than an actual life, a literary artifact that can never be a definitive or wholly accurate record, precisely because the biographer is always being forced to make choices – and, no less than any other writer, he will sometimes make good choices and sometimes bad ones. What we can never escape, in any biography, is the biographer's presence, just as we can never escape the novelist in the novel. But this is just as inevitable as the fact that the path to understanding a novel, a painting, a symphony, lies through an understanding of the human being who produced it as well as through the human being who is trying to understand it. It is the first of these human beings – the producer, the artist – the post-modernists wish to be rid of. The historian and the biographer know that assessments of both the sitter and the artist are necessary components of any commentary on the work itself and of the quality of the critical conclusions reached about it. Surely Professor Nadel is right to say, as he does, that the biographer, if he fails, should blame his own faulty application of the biographical method, his deficiencies of talent and sensibility, rather than the method itself.

As fallible as biography may sometimes be, I consider it a more reliable route to the possible meanings of what a writer has written than the approach of those, like the post-modernists, who write autobiography when they talk about the reader's relation to the text and omit the author from consideration. Of course criticism which is primarily about itself is going to find it difficult to locate meaning outside of itself – in, for example, the work, let alone the life. The good historian/biographer understands the problems of excessive subjectivity and tries to avoid or minimize them. Since, for the post-modernists, there is no discoverable objective truth or meaning in a text, they do not look for it; instead they poke around through the farther reaches of their own psyches, which is why they are at the same time so incomprehensible and so dull.

IV

Obviously my interest is in the subject the post-modernists have tried to abolish – or, as they like to say, elide – the subject we as readers shall always have with us: the author. He may have suffered a temporary death in the 1970s and 1980s; he is being reborn in the 1990s. One has only to look at the explosion of public interest in biography, autobiography, diaries, letters, and journals these days to see the author being resurrected. In its various forms, history is being read in the 1990s more than any other *genre*.

In ignoring the author, in supposing him or her not to be present, is assuming that, for example, novels are objective dramatizations composed by invisible persons who are not necessarily telling a story but only writing something indistinguishable from a wall poster or a legal contract, the post-modernists have not only distorted the profession of criticism beyond recognition; they have also tried to take away from reading one of its great pleasures, the pleasure of getting to know the author. Why do people so often progress, one after another, through the works of a particular author, once discovered? The answer is clear. It is because his books are like no one else's; they appeal to the reader in such a way as to give him unique enjoyment. We search out the works of some authors rather than those of others not so much because of the works themselves but rather because of the name on the title-page – the very thing Foucault wishes to expunge. When someone goes into a bookshop and asks for the latest Updike or the latest le Carré, or inquires if yet another novel by Trollope is in paperback, she is asking, of course, for the author, a known quantity, rather than for the text, which until actually read is unknown to her except indirectly through other works with the same name on the title-page; one tends not to look forward quite so hungrily to a new critical commentary. The reader opens the novel assuming that she will read on to the end because she has enjoyed the author's other books. This, after all, is the way in which the vast majority of people who read do read. No one whose object in reading is pleasure will ask for the newest wall poster, the latest thing in legal contracts, or the most recent deconstructive commentary. To talk about a novel without talking about the author is to omit this crucial aspect of one's experience in reading novels: the personality of the novelist.

As Wayne Booth has argued in *The Rhetoric of Fiction*, the reader knows – he cannot help knowing – that he is being told a story by someone. Who the author is determines what he writes and how he tells his story, and so also determines in large measure the way in which the reader is likely to respond to it. We come to an undeniable fact about all novels: they are told by an implied author, who is created by the biographical author and is necessarily part of the formal experience of reading the novel. You cannot talk about form without talking about authors.

In letters, diaries, notebooks, in any conscious form of autobiography, there will be some holding back by the writer. An autobiography can distort; facts can be realigned or omitted. But fiction never lies; it reveals the writer totally. Conrad knew this well enough. 'A writer of imaginative prose . . . stands confessed in his work,' he declared in *A Personal Record* (1912). 'He stands there, the only reality in an invented world, among imaginary things, happenings and people. Writing about them, he is only writing about himself. . . . Indeed, everyone who puts pen to paper . . . can speak of nothing else.' In 'The Critic as Artist,' Wilde reminds us that 'Man is least himself when he talks in his own person. Give him a mask, and he will tell you the truth.' And Samuel Butler admits this readily enough in *The Way of All Flesh*. 'Every man's work, whether it be literature or music or pictures or architecture or anything else,' Butler declares, 'is always a portrait of himself, and the more he tries to conceal himself the more clearly will his character appear in spite of him.'

All fiction emerges from the consciousness of the writer and is therefore shaped in the way that consciousness perceives. Seen in this light, novelists, perhaps, are the only people who tell the truth. Furthermore, the writer's perceptions and his consciousness necessarily will be deeply involved in the shared assumptions of his culture, even if he rejects them. Wilde's famous assertion that Life imitates Art rather than vice versa reflects his understanding that art is always a product of the artist and a reflection of his personality.

Somerset Maugham reminds us in *Ten Novels and Their Authors* that the novelist is always at the mercy of his own bias. The subjects he chooses, the characters he invents, and his attitudes toward them are conditioned by that bias. 'Whatever he writes is the expression of his personality and it is the manifestation of his innate instincts, his feeling and his experience. However hard he tries to be objective, he remains the slave of his idiosyncrasies.' However hard he tries to be impartial, he cannot help taking sides. If we ask what is it that must be combined with the creative instinct to make it possible for a writer to produce a work of value, the answer must be: personality. The writer sees things in a manner peculiar to himself. Even the most ferocious 'realist' does not merely 'copy' life: he arranges it to suit his purpose, whatever that may be. A man or a woman who writes a great work is nonetheless a man or a woman. 'I do not believe that they are right who say that the defects of famous [writers] should be ignored,' Maugham has written. 'I think it is better that we should know them [that is, the defects]. Then, though we are conscious of having faults as glaring as theirs, we can believe that that is no hindrance to our achieving also something of their virtues.'

Maugham suggests that biography can be as great an instrument for the achievement of what the Victorians called 'moral realism' as any novel by George Eliot or Trollope, and I am inclined to agree with him. Henry James actually thought of his novels as biographies, as the 'true histories' of 'real' men and women. Our knowledge that Beethoven was a nasty character cannot diminish our appreciation of his music; on the contrary, it may teach us that even those who, like ourselves, are flawed, can achieve something – in spite of, or perhaps because of, their flaws. In this way biography can make art more accessible, more understandable, to wider audiences.

The artist, says Maugham in *The Summing Up*, produces what he produces for the liberation of his soul. 'If the artist is a novelist, he uses experience of people and places, apprehension of the self, loves and hates, deepest thoughts, passing fancies, to draw, in one work after another, a picture of life. It can never be more than a partial one, but if he is honest he cannot help, in the end, doing something else as well: he will draw a picture of himself.'

Thomas Hardy defines art as the pattern in things perceived by the artist. Just as the painter thinks with his brush and his colors, the novelist thinks with his story and his characters; his view of life, though he may be unconscious of it, his personality, exists as a series of invented human actions.

As Maugham says, people are sometimes outraged at discovering, as so often happens when a biography is published, the discrepancies between an artist's life and his work. They have not been able to reconcile Beethoven's idealism and his meanness of spirit, Wagner's inspiration with his selfishness and dishonesty, Cervantes' moral obliquity with his tenderness and magnanimity, Jane Austen's wonderful wit with her cold-heartedness and malice, Hardy's great poetry with his monumental selfishness and mendacity, Dickens's comic genius with the sheer malevolence of the man, Tennyson's public purity with his private vices. Sometimes, in their post-lapsurian indignation, people have sought to persuade themselves that the work of such men and women could not possess the value they once thought it possessed. When it has been brought to their attention that great poets have left behind them a large body of obscene verse, that extollers of the domestic virtues such as Coventry Patmore collected pornography, or that so apparently pure a novelist as Edith Wharton was subject to fantasies of incest, they have been horrified. They have an uneasy feeling that the whole life was a sham and either accuse their idols of humbug or the biographers of meddling in areas they should have left alone. However, the artist, as Maugham says in *Ten Novels and Their Authors*, is not one person but many. It is because he is many people that he can create many people, and perhaps one measure of his greatness is the number of selves he comprises. When a writer fashions a character that does not carry conviction it is usually because there is in himself nothing of that person; he has had to fall back either on observation or research, and so has described rather than begotten.

V

There is no such thing as being impervious to history. We live in the midst of our own historical moment; our values, our thoughts, our prejudices, our perceptions, are products of that historical moment and of the accumulated wisdom of social history as inevitably as they are products of our unique psyche. Whatever a man or woman may choose to do, two of the reasons for that choice must always be found in the personality and in the moment. The personality and the moment permit and encourage certain responses to certain situations while discouraging others; and a person's actions are seen by others as either appropriate or inappropriate, depending upon contemporary values and taste. Every age reasons from different premises. Alexander the Great is considered by some modern historians a vicious barbarian; in his time the acquisition of as much land as possible by whatever means necessary was the prime measure of a great leader. Everyone deserves to be judged by the standards of his own day. We cannot help being conditioned by our milieu; and so it follows that the more we study history the more likely we are to be able to assess wisely the actions of the dead.

History used to be studied as a mirror of the present, a glass in which one could see reflected the meaning of the past and the probable course of the future. One can study it still for the same reasons. The trappings of our lives – our houses, our books, our means of communication and travel – these things may change, but our essential natures remain conditioned by the forces of the age we live in. This is always true. What is worked upon is always changing, as a direct result of what is working on it; human nature itself is an artifact of history and can be studied that way. And by history I do not mean the chronological record only, but the history of taste, the history of values, the history, above all, of ideas.

We seem to study social and intellectual history less and less these days, though our interest in literary personalities is obviously waxing rather than waning. We should never forget that all works of art are products of a unique mind, and that that mind can be studied if we know how to obtain the tools for studying it; that the time in which that mind existed can be studied if we know how to study it; and that the impact of the time upon the mind can be assessed if we know how to assess it. I think that some of us in the profession of literary criticism have forgotten how to do some of these things.

It would seem that historical and biographical approaches to literature are making a comeback of sorts in the 1990s as the purely textual schools of criticism become increasingly discredited. Derrida believes in a writing without presence, without history, without cause, which does not connect with anything, which has no subject and no theme and no purpose. But such writing, if it existed, would be just babble, a ground without a figure, a margin without a page of text. No wonder deconstruction survives today largely in the form of self-parody. To deconstruct something is to kill it, to make it disappear, to force it to commit suicide. So the ultimate goal of deconstruction would seem to be the disappearance of art.

In his play *The Pressure Cooker*, David Lodge describes the sort of novel most ideally suited to post-modern criticism: an introduction, followed by 250 blank pages. Lodge's point is the same as mine: it is time to put the author and the real – as over against the deconstructed – text back into literary studies. And so good-night, Jacques, good-night, Michel; good-night, Roland, and Stanley, and Hillis, and Paul, and Geoffrey, and Murray. Write if you get work.

Notes

Notes to the Preface   *Dale Salwak*

1. Lytton Strachey, *Eminent Victorians* (New York, 1963) p. vi.
2. See Stephen B. Oates (ed.), 'Prologue,' *Biography as High Adventure* (Amherst, Mass., 1986) p. xi; Justin Kaplan, 'The "Real Life",' *ibid.*, p. 70.
3. Quoted by Steve Weinberg, 'Biography: Telling the Untold Story,' *The Writer*, CVI (1993) 25.
4. Quoted by Patricia Bosworth, 'The Mysterious Art of Biography,' *The Writer*, CIII (1990) 18.
5. Catherine Drinker Bowen, *Biography: The Craft and the Calling* (Boston, Mass., and Toronto, 1969) p. xii.
6. Dr Judith Priestman to Dale Salwak, reprinted *Times Literary Supplement*, 22 April 1994, p. 17.
7. John Updike, 'The Man Within,' *The New Yorker*, 26 June and 3 July 1995, p. 187.
8. Quoted by Weinberg, *op. cit.*, p. 23; Meryle Secrest, 'The Story of a Life,' *The Writer*, June 1981, p. 12; Leon Edel, *Writing Lives: Principia Biographica* (New York and London, 1984), p. 33.

Notes to Chapter 1: A Culture of Biography   *Justin Kaplan*

1. James Boswell, *Boswell's Life of Johnson* (London, 1904) I, p. 22.
2. Samuel Coleridge, *Biographia Literaria* (1817), ed. J. Shawcross (London, 1907) I, pp. 27–8.
3. Lytton Strachey, *Eminent Victorians* (New York, 1963) p. vi.
4. C. Wright Mills, *The Sociological Imagination* (New York, 1959) p. 6.
5. Walt Whitman, 'Preface 1855,' in Harold W. Blodgett and Sculley Bradley (eds), *Leaves of Grass* (New York, 1965) p. 713.
6. Quoted by Ernest Samuels in his *Henry Adams: The Major Phase* (Cambridge, Mass., 1964) p. 155.
7. Quoted by Carolyn Heilbrun in her *Writing a Woman's Life* (New York, 1988) p. 28.
8. Julian Barnes, *Flaubert's Parrot* (New York, 1985) p. 31.
9. Marcel Proust, *Contre Saint-Beuve* (New York, 1958) pp. 99–100, 104.

10. Virginia Woolf in Nigel Nicolson (ed.), *Letters of Virginia Woolf* (New York, 1978) III, p. 474.
11. See Ewen Montagu, *The Man Who Never Was* (New York, 1954).
12. Louise Brooks, *Lulu in Hollywood* (New York, 1982) p. 74.

Notes to Chapter 3: Those Wonderful Youths and Maidens, My Reviewers *N. John Hall*

1. John Powell, *Magill Book Reviews* for *Dow Jones/Retrieval*, 1992.
2. C.A. Latimer, 'The Irish Question,' *The American Scholar*, LXI (1992) 620.
3. David Lyons, review in *The American Spectator*, 25 April 1992, p. 68.
4. Roger Kimball, 'A Novelist Who Hunted the Fox: Anthony Trollope Today,' *The New Criterion*, March 1992, p. 18.
5. John Halperin, review in *Biography*, XV (1992) 419.
6. Kimball, *op. cit.*, p. 18.
7. R.D. McMaster, review in *Victorian Review*, XVIII (1992) 87.
8. Kimball, *op. cit.*, p. 18.
9. R.C. Terry, review in *Victorian Studies*, XXXVI (1992) 110–11.
10. N. John Hall, *Trollope: A Biography* (Oxford, 1991) p. xv.
11. Kimball, *op. cit.*, p. 18.
12. Terry, *op. cit.*, p. 110.
13. John Powell, *op. cit.*
14. Hugh David, 'Minister of Stateliness,' *The Times Saturday Review*, 9 November 1991, p. 47.
15. McMaster, *op. cit.*, pp. 85–7.
16. Walter Kendrick, 'Parallel Lives: The State of the Art of Literary Biography,' *Voice Literary Supplement*, March 1992, p. 12.
17. Thomas Hardy in Richard Little Purdy and Michael Millgate (eds), *The Collected Letters of Thomas Hardy* (Oxford, 1982) III, p. 266.

Notes to Chapter 4: The Necrophiliac Art? *Martin Stannard*

1. Roy Campbell, *Nation and Athenæum*, 19 May 1928, p. 212; reprinted Martin Stannard (ed.), *Evelyn Waugh: The Critical Heritage* (London, 1984), p. 72.
2. Evelyn Waugh, *Rossetti: His Life and Works* (London, 1928), p.12.
3. *Ibid.*, p. 12.

4. Joyce Carol Oates, 'A Humane and Adventurous Art,' *Dialogue*, XVIII (1979) 98.
5. Michael Holroyd, 'Literary Biography,' *Literature Matters* (Newsletter of the British Council's Literature Department), no. 9 (1991) 4–5; 4.
6. *Ibid.*, p. 4.
7. *Ibid.*, p. 5.
8. Sean Haldane, 'Hardy,' *Times Literary Supplement*, 1 April 1994, p.15; Hynes's review was published in the *TLS* on 18 March 1994.
9. For an exposition on these difficulties see Janet Malcolm, 'Annals of Biography: The Silent Woman,' *The New Yorker*, 23 and 30 August 1993, pp. 82–125, 128–39, 142–59; adapted as *The Silent Woman: Sylvia Plath and Ted Hughes* (New York, 1994).
10. Germaine Greer, 'Me, My Work, My Friends, and My Parasite,' *Guardian*, 31 October 1994, p. 18.
11. Malcolm, *op. cit.*, p. 86.
12. *Ibid.*
13. Greer, *op. cit.*, p. 18.
14. *Ibid.*
15. Quoted by Oates, *op. cit.*, p. 97.
16. George Eliot to John Blackwood (20 February 1874) in Gordon S. Haight (ed.), *The George Eliot Letters*, vol. VI: *1874–1877* (New Haven, Conn., 1956) p. 23.
17. Quoted by Malcolm, *op. cit.*, p. 128.
18. *Ibid.*, p. 113.
19. Paul Johnson, *Sunday Telegraph*, 19 April, 1992.
20. Philip Camaran, *Literary Review*, May 1992.
21. *Times Educational Supplement*, 1 May 1992.
22. Quoted by Oates, *op. cit.*, p. 97.

Notes to Chapter 5: Read That Countenance Catherine Aird

1. Harold Osborne (ed.), *Oxford Companion to Art* (Oxford, 1970) p. 66.
2. Horace Walpole in G. Vertue (ed.), *Anecdotes of Painting in England* (London, 1763) III, ch. 1.
3. Aubrey C. Kail, *The Medical Mind of Shakespeare* (Balgowlah, Australia, 1986) pp. 9, 13.
4. Quoted by Dr Theodore Dalrymple, *The Spectator*, 20 June 1992, p. 128.

5. Sir Edward Grey, 'The Pleasures of Reading,' *Letters: The Journal of the Royal Society of Literature* (1994) 27. Reprint of an address delivered 21 May 1924.
6. Charlotte Brontë, *Villette* (London, 1967) ch. 7, p. 61.

Notes to Chapter 8: The Red Room: Stephen Crane and Me
Linda H. Davis

1. Mark Barr, 'The Haunted House of Brede,' in 'Stephen Crane Remembered,' *Studies in American Fiction*, IV (1976) 45–64.
2. Stanley Wertheim and Paul Sorrentino (eds), *The Correspondence of Stephen Crane* (New York, 1988) p. 198.
3. *Ibid.*, p. 161.
4. Karl Edwin Harriman, 'A Romantic Idealist – Mr Stephen Crane,' *The Literary Review*, IV (1900) 85–7; Hamlin Garland, 'Stephen Crane as I Knew Him,' reprinted in *The Yale Review*, LXXVII (1985) 12.
5. Wertheim and Sorrentino, *op. cit.*, p. 507.
6. *Ibid.*, pp. 515, 504.
7. Quoted in *New York Journal*, 17 September 1896.
8. J.C. Levenson in Fredson Bowers (ed.), *The University of Virginia Edition of the Works of Stephen Crane* (Charlottesville, 1969) v, p. cviii.
9. Quoted in Stanley Wertheim and Paul Sorrentino (eds), *The Crane Log: A Documentary Life of Stephen Crane 1871–1900* (New York, 1994) p. 442.

Notes to Chapter 9: Discovering Kingsley Amis   *Dale Salwak*

1. Leon Edel, *Writing Lives: Principia Biographica* (New York, 1984) p. 150; Catherine Drinker Bowen, *Biography: The Craft and the Calling* (Boston and Toronto, 1969) p. 43.
2. David Spark, 'Amis Turns to Unlucky Stanley,' *Northern Echo*, 25 May 1984, p. 13.
3. Michael Murphy, 'Is Amis Unfair to Fair Sex?' *Sunday Independent*, 27 May 1984, p. 15.
4. Leon Edel, *op. cit.*, p. 107.
5. Kingsley Amis, *Memoirs* (London, 1991) p. xv.
6. Edward Wasiolek (ed.), *Dostoevsky: The Notebooks for Crime and Punishment* (Chicago, 1967) p. xi.

7. *Ibid.*
8. Kingsley Amis, Notebook for *That Uncertain Feeling,* Harry Ransom Humanities Research Center, University of Texas, Austin.
9. Kingsley Amis to Dale Salwak, 16 October 1986. Amis used this passage as an epigraph to his essay 'Communication and the Victorian Poet,' *Essays in Criticism* IV (1954) 386–99.
10. James Phelan, *Beyond the Tenure Track* (Columbus, 1991) p. 101.
11. Kingsley Amis to Dale Salwak, 30 January 1973, from a letter to Madame S. M. Haimart.

Notes to Chapter 10: Spinning Straw into Gold *Diane Wood Middlebrook*

1. Denise Levertov, 'Anne Sexton: Light Up the Cave,' *Light Up the Cave* (New York, 1981) p. 80.
2. Scott Donaldson, "Writing the Cheever,' *Sewanee Review,* XCVIII (1990), 527–45.

Notes to Chapter 12: Private and Public Lives *Natasha Spender*

1. A list of errors of fact by the late © Stephen Spender is deposited in the British Library and the New York Public Library.
2. See Christopher Isherwood, *Christopher and His Kind* (London and New York, 1976) and Stephen Spender, *World within World* (London and New York, 1951).
3. Neville Braybrooke (ed.), *Letters of J.R. Ackerley* (London, 1975).

Notes to Chapter 13: Mather, Poe, Houdini *Kenneth Silverman*

1. Martha Wolfenstein, 'How is Mourning Possible?,' *Psychoanalytic Study of the Child,* XXI (1966) 93–122; 'Loss, Rage, and Repetition,' *Psychoanalytic Study of the Child,* XXIV (1969) 432–60; 'The Image of the Lost Parent,' *Psychoanalytic Study of the Child,* XXVIII (1973) 433–56.
2. James A. Harrison (ed.), *The Complete Works of Edgar Allan Poe,* vol. XVII (1902; repr. New York, 1979) p. 437.
3. Henry James, *The Princess Casamassima* (1886; Harmondsworth, England, 1977) pp. 13, 9.

172 *Notes*

4. Jonathan Richardson, *The Works of Jonathan Richardson* (London, 1792) p. 12.
5. For biographers whose work involves extensive historical research, many benefits of electric information-webs have been neutralized by new copyright laws. Beyond ill-defined 'fair use,' the laws virtually forbid the use of manuscript material. They do so by granting perpetual copyright to the author's descendants through however-many generations. Preposterously, they recognise no difference between letters written by Virginia Woolf and, say, Genghis Khan. In both cases the biographer must obtain permission from the descendants in order to quote. He becomes a tracer of lost persons, only to at last locate a surviving great-great-great-grandnephew who couldn't care less. Pity the historical biographer who uses manuscript material to also build up secondary characters. However obscure or long dead they may be, he must search out the descendants of them all – work for a full-time team of genealogists. Intimidated by the new laws, some major repositories now refuse to even photocopy manuscripts without prior permission, though the documents be 150 or more years old.

   Perversely, while more biographical material is more readily available today than at any earlier time, much less can be explored and used. The copyright statutes must be revised so as to distinguish between recent manuscripts of commercial value to immediate heirs, and manuscripts of historical value by persons long gone and sometimes little-known. Until then, historical biographers and their publishers have no choice but to flout the law or be forced out of the biography business.
6. Quoted in Michael Wreszin, *A Rebel In Defense of Tradition: The Life and Politics of Dwight Macdonald* (New York, 1994) p. 488.

Notes to Chapter 17: Sharing the Role: The Biographer as Sleuth
Margaret Lewis

1. Ngaio Marsh, 'My Poor Boy,' broadcast on *Bookshop*, Radio New Zealand, 1 January 1957.
2. John Walsh, 'Death Becomes Her,' *The Independent on Sunday*, 22 October 1994, p. 38.
3. H.R.F. Keating, *Writing Crime Fiction* (London, 1986) p. 2.
4. John G. Cawelti, *Adventure, Mystery and Romance* (Chicago, Ill.,

1976) p. 137.
5. Julian Symons, *Bloody Murder*, revised edn (London, 1985) p. 66.
6. Ngaio Marsh, *Black Beech and Honeydew*, revised edn (Auckland, 1981) p. 305.
7. Elaine Budd, *13 Mistresses of Murder* (New York, 1986) p. 68.
8. Thomas de Quincey, 'On Murder Considered as One of the Fine Arts,' in David Masson (ed.), *Select Essays* (Edinburgh, 1928) p. 13.
9. Sue Feder, 'Ellis Peters,' in L. Henderson (ed.), *Twentieth-Century Crime and Mystery Writers*, 3rd edn (Chicago, Ill., 1991) p. 848.
10. Symons, *op. cit.*, p. 210.

Related Works

Aaron, Daniel (ed.), *Studies in Biography* (Cambridge, Mass., 1978).

Alpern, Sara, *et al.* (eds), *The Challenge of Feminist Biography: Writing the Lives of Modern American Women* (Urbana, Ill., 1992).

Altick, Richard D., *Lives and Letters: A History of Literary Biography in England and America* (New York, 1966).

Ascher, Carol, *et al.* (eds), *Between Women: Biographers, Novelists, Teachers, and Artists Write about their Work on Women* (Boston, Mass., 1984).

Baron, Samuel H., and Carl Pletsch (eds), *Introspection in Biography: The Biographer's Quest for Self-Awareness* (Hillsdale, N.J., 1985).

Batchelor, John (ed.), *The Art of Literary Biography* (Oxford, 1995).

Beales, Derek, *History and Biography* (Cambridge, England, 1981).

Bell, Susan Groag, and Marilyn Yalom (eds), *Revealing Lives: Autobiography, Biography, and Gender* (Albany, N.Y., 1993).

Berry, Thomas Elliot (ed.), *The Biographer's Craft* (New York, 1967).

Bowen, Catherine Drinker, *Adventures of a Biographer* (Boston, Mass., 1959).

Bradford, Gamaliel, *Biography and the Human Heart* (Boston, Mass., 1932).

Clifford, James L., *Biography as an Art: Selected Criticism, 1560–1960* (New York, 1962).

——, *From Puzzles to Portraits: Problems of a Literary Biographer* (Chapel Hill, N.C., 1970).

Cole, John Y. (ed.), *Biography and Books* (Washington, D.C., 1986).

Coltrera. Joseph T. (ed.), *Lives, Events, and Other Players: Directions in Psychobiography* (New York, 1981).

Denzin, Norman K., *Interpretive Biography* (Newbury Park, Cal., 1989).

Donaldson, Ian, *et al.* (eds), *Shaping Lives: Reflections on Biography* (Canberra, 1992).

Edel, Leon, *Writing Lives: Principia Biographica* (New York, 1984).

Ellmann, Richard, *Golden Codgers: Biographical Speculations* (London, 1973).

Empson, William, *Using Biography* (Cambridge, Mass., 1984).

Epstein, William H. (ed.), *Contesting the Subject: Essays in Postmodern Theory and Practice of Biography and Biographical Criticism* (West Lafayette, Ind., 1991).

Friedson, Anthony M., *New Directions in Biography* (Honolulu, 1981).

Fromm, Gloria (ed.), *Essaying Biography: A Celebration of Leon Edel* (Honolulu, 1986).

Garraty, John A., *The Nature of Biography* (New York, 1957).

Gittelson, Brenda, *Biography* (New York, 1991).

——, *The Self-Portrait of a Literary Biographer* (Athens, Ga., 1994).

Gittings, Robert, *The Nature of Biography* (Seattle, Wash., 1978).

Halperin, John, *Novelists in Their Youth* (New York, 1990).

Hamilton, Ian, *In Search of J.D. Salinger* (New York, 1988).

——, *Keepers of the Flame: Literary Estates and the Rise of Biography* (London, 1992).

Handlin, Oscar, *Truth in History* (Cambridge, Mass., 1979).

Holmes, Richard, *Footsteps: Adventures of a Romantic Biographer* (New York, 1985; repr. Harmondsworth, 1986).

Homberger, Eric, and John Charmley (eds), *The Troubled Face of Biography* (London, 1988).

Honan, Park, *Author's Lives: On Literary Biography and the Arts of Language* (New York, 1990).

Iles, Teresa (ed.), *All Sides of the Subject: Women and Biography* (New York, 1992).

Kallich, Martin, *The Psychological Milieu of Lytton Strachey* (New York, 1961).

Kendall, Paul Murray, *The Art of Biography* (New York, 1965).

Lomask, Milton, *The Biographer's Craft* (New York, 1986).

McAdams, Dan P., and Richard L. Ochberg (eds), *Psychobiography and Life Narratives* (Durham, N.C., 1988).

Malcolm, Janet, *The Silent Woman: Sylvia Plath and Ted Hughes* (New York, 1994).

Mandell, Gail Porter (ed.), *Life into Art: Conversations with Seven Contemporary Biographers* (Fayetteville, Ark., 1991).

Maurois, Andre, *Aspects of Biography* (New York, 1929).

Meyers, Jeffrey (ed.), *The Craft of Literary Biography* (New York, 1985).

——, *The Spirit of Biography* (Ann Arbor, Mich., 1989).

Moraitis, George, and George H. Pollock (eds), *Psychoanalytic Studies of Biography* (Madison, Conn., 1987).

Nadel, Ira Bruce, *Biography: Fiction, Fact, and Form* (New York, 1984).

Novarr, David, *The Lines of Life: Theories of Biography, 1880–1970* (West Lafayette, Ind., 1986).

Oates, Stephen B. (ed.), *Biography as High Adventure: Life-Writers Speak on Their Art* (Amherst, Mass., 1986).

O'Connor, Ulick, *Biographers and the Art of Biography* (London, 1993).

Pachter, Marc (ed.), *Telling Lives: The Biographer's Art* (Washington, D.C., 1979).

Powers, Lyall H. (ed.), *Leon Edel and Literary Art* (Ann Arbor, Mich., 1988).

Reid, B.L., *Necessary Lives: Biographical Reflections* (Columbia, D.C., 1990).

Rollyson, Carl, *Biography: An Annotated Bibliography* (Pasadena, Calif., and Englewood Cliffs, N.J., 1992).

Runyon, William McKinley, *Life Histories and Psychobiography: Explorations in Theory and Method* (New York, 1984).

Schellinger, Paul E. (ed.), *St James Guide to Biography* (Chicago, Ill., 1991).

Shelston, Alan, *Biography* (London, 1977).

Stone, Irving, *The Science, and the Art, of Biography* (Los Angeles, Calif., 1986).

Strachey, Lytton, *Eminent Victorians* (New York, 1963).

Symons, A.J.A., *The Quest for Corvo: An Experiment in Biography* (Baltimore, Md, 1940).

Veninga, James F. (ed.), *The Biographer's Gift: Life Histories and Humanism* (College Station, Tx., 1983).

Wagner-Martin, Linda, *Telling Women's Lives: The New Biography* (New Brunswick, N.J., 1994).

Walter, James and Raija Nugent (eds), *Biographers at Work* (Queensland, Australia, 1984).

Ward, Wilfred, *Last Lectures by Wilfred Ward* (Freeport, N.Y., 1967).

Whittemore, Reed, *Whole Lives: Shapers of Modern Biography* (Baltimore, Md, 1989).

Zinsser, William (ed.), *Extraordinary Lives: The Art and Craft of American Biography* (Boston, Mass., 1986).

Index